a journey to the heart

Capturing the Spirit

of Global Education

a compilation of essays

by

The Learning Community

Published by

Rainbow Bridge, Palo Alto, California

a journey to the heart
Capturing the Spirit of Global Education
a compilation of essays
by The Learning Community

Published by
Rainbow Bridge
823 Forest Avenue
Palo Alto, CA 94301

Other Rainbow Bridge books:

ESSENTIAL EDUCATION: Drawing Forth the Golden Child
by Gary Bacon, Ph. D.

Production notes:

Camera ready art and text for the production of this book were created on an IBM® compatible computer and a Canon LBP-Mark III Laser Printer, using Ventura Publisher® software. Photostats were made from the laser printed copy and printed on an offset printer.

Notice: all profits resulting from the publishing of the first edition of this book were used to fund the Kenyan service projects that were established by The Learning Community.

About the cover:

A young Kikuyu girl invites her guests to share the hospitality of her family's small farm. The expression *"Karibuni Kenya!"* (You are welcome in Kenya!) epitomizes this journey. The photograph was taken by Megan Mathias.

Dedication:

We wish to dedicate this book to the two groups that made our venture possible: our generous families, friends, and neighbors in the United States who supported our vision to go to Kenya, and the proud people of Kenya who opened their hearts and homes to our group and welcomed us as family.

We used the rainbow as our symbol of world goodwill as we sought support for our trip. It was our privilege to carry that symbol, as a Peace Wreath, to the other side of the world and to have it accepted, so whole-heartedly, by the people we met in Kenya.

The spirit of service took on a new meaning to us as we experienced the joy in people's hearts around the world. We found that true service was equally inspirational to everyone involved; that, in those moments when we reached the level of true service, the role of the giver and receiver blurred, and everyone became as one.

Table of Contents

CHAPTER 1: PREPARING FOR THE JOURNEY

CHAPTER 2: EXPLORING THE INNER CITY

CHAPTER 3: LIVING WITH THE KIKUYU

CHAPTER 4: OVERCOMING ALL BARRIERS

CHAPTER 5: JOINING IN WITH THE MAASAI

CHAPTER 6: REFLECTING ON THE JOURNEY

Acknowledgments:

The journey described in the following pages resulted from the efforts of two groups of Learning Community students over two academic years. The first group set up the experiences that led to the decision to go to Kenya; the subsequent group planned and carried out the trip. Seven students were in both groups.

Individuals outside of our group who contributed significant time, energy, or inspiration to our venture included Susan Beaudry, Nancy Estill, Steven McCormick, David Maina, and Sandra Mardigian. We are eternally grateful to each of these generous and thoughtful human beings.

The writing project that produced this book succeeded because the students were willing to write their personal accounts of the adventures they shared on their journey. The students willingly submitted their works to the scrutiny of their peers, and diligently worked and reworked their essays.

Leah Mowery and Jonathan Tourzan graciously took the individual essays and sequenced, edited, and refined them. Jonathan also wrote the connecting theme pieces that gave the stories better continuity, and he spent two weeks of his summer vacation helping edit and rewrite the students' contributions.

Chris Wells provided valuable editing advice and generous encouragement. Colette Danner helped critique the work-in-progress. Cynthia Sun advised on layout and style and helped proofread. Gary Bacon provided the computer equipment, did the layout, edited obsessively, and oversaw the project.

In the final analysis, the students' enthusiasm, commitment, and vision were the driving forces behind this venture.

Forethought

As you reflect on the stories that follow, we invite you to consider the question of what is important and valuable in education. And, as we bring you into contact with our group's learning experiences, we ask that you turn your attention to the larger issue of what is important and valuable in the world. Clearly, the two questions inherently connect. The collection of essays that follow dramatically illustrates this connection, since they grew out of our hands-on, educational experiences in the world.

The power of the educational process that shaped these writings deserves further elaboration. We offer you the following perspectives to help you gain a better understand of the experiences we shared and the insights we gained in our journey to Kenya.

Three fundamental assumptions lie at the base of this work. The first premise is that the delicate social fabric and the ecological support system of the planet are in grave danger. Problems increase as population and technology grow exponentially and move on a collision course through time.

Secondly, we, as members of the human family, must reflect on the ramifications of our actions that affect the social and environmental welfare of the planet. We must make significant adjustments in our lifestyles so that we live more in harmony with the world. Each succeeding generation of human beings must leave the earth in better condition than its predecessor did. Then we can begin to ensure that all living things on the planet can enjoy the highest quality of life.

The third assumption underlying this work is that the process of education must be an active instrument of change in the world. To educate our citizenry in a truly global sense, we must engage people in a process of effective, creative change. This process must include active research, hands-on development of solutions to world problems, and a deliberate pursuit of global consciousness.

The challenge of creative change in the world is great. Conservationist John Muir once said, "when we try to pick out anything by itself, we find it hitched to everything else in the universe." Assuming that this assertion is true, we must move wisely and deliberately into the world of change. Mindless tampering or short-sighted solutions may result in even greater harm to our world than current practices.

On the other hand, given the current accelerated rate of change in the world, we must act quickly and decisively. We must prevent the erosion of the delicate balance of forces in our universe. To delay appropriate action or to become mired in debate is a luxury that we cannot afford.

To bring the issue of effective, creative change into classrooms around the world, we need to make an important shift in the way we view the world. We must learn to understand the dynamics of change from a global perspective. We must own our responsibility to this dynamic. Most importantly, we must believe in our power to make a difference—before it is too late.

To treat our youth as simply passive receptors of information ignores and wastes a tremendously vital resource for the world. This mind set also encourages passivity in the minds and hearts of our youth. It leaves little more than pleasure-seeking as an alternative for young people in terms of their making an active statement in the world. Our approach embraces the premise that to be truly educated, one must be empowered as a co-creator of the world.

We offer the development of our travel experience to Kenya as a real-world example of these philosophical ideals. These stories grew out of our experience as a *community of learners*, which is the basis of our Learning Community. Being a holistic educational program, we have the opportunity to integrate the physical, emotional, intellectual, societal, environmental, and spiritual domains into a comprehensive curriculum.

We actively involve our students both in the development of their studies and in the administration of their program. We coordinate our individual academic studies through a personal contract that our teacher approves and monitors. We co-create our group studies in the framework of shared decision-making in community meetings. The teacher becomes a member of the community and shares responsibility for its success with the students.

The program has been operating successfully since a group of students, parents, and teachers presented its developmental proposal to the local school board in the early seventies. The proposal grew out of a desire by its members to supplement the regular curriculum of the high school. This group wished to provide a sense of continuity and motivation in an institution that they perceived to be disjointed and to hold little personal meaning for students. They also sought to ground their academic work in direct experiences in the world.

The Learning Community, in its present form, involves a group of twenty-five students and their teacher in a special program within a public high school in Los Altos, California. The students spend a minimum of four hours together each school day, using this forum in which to develop their studies throughout the year. It is an open model that varies from one year to the next, depending on student needs and interests, teacher input, and world events.

Our curriculum at both the individual and group levels is created through a process of goal setting. This process encourages commitment to well-developed goals and objectives, direct involvement in experiences, and periodic group and individual reflections and evaluations; consequently, program development incorporates program improvement.

From this platform, we address three fundamental questions: "How can I better understand and direct the inner forces that make me who I am?"; "How can I develop healthy working relationships with people and organizations?"; and "What is valuable and necessary for me to learn so that I may become a contributing, world citizen?"

These questions lead us to exciting outcomes. We engage in rigorous self-examination, the development of close interpersonal relationships, and the development of effective organizational skills. As we look to the external world, we gain an understanding of the patterns and dynamics inherent in social and environmental issues. Next, we develop strategies for change in the world. Through this process, we develop a sense of responsible ownership and stewardship for the planet.

This claim is more than theoretical, as you will see in the accounts that we have assembled in this book. The experiences we shared are a living testimony that this process of education can be highly effective. We also are confident that a similar process can be effective for others who are willing to apply themselves to the task.

Within the context of The Learning Community, we made several decisions that resulted in our journey to Kenya. As an action component of our program, students in two different academic years funded water projects in Nepal and in Kenya. They conducted cultural, historical, and economic research into these countries. They also met with and learned from visitors to the United States from these countries. Insights gained from these experiences seeded a desire in the group to travel and to engage in further cultural interactions and service projects.

Each year, a group of our students returns to our program for a second year. Thus, some ideas or projects can grow and progress in ensuing years. This year, our returning students wanted to know more about Kenya and desired more involvement with its people. This motivated our new students to build on the interest and commitment of their predecessors. Eventually, they all worked together to carry out the journey described in this book.

Our intense level of commitment was a direct result of our involvement in the process of our own learning. Education became real for us because we helped shape our education. We saw the concrete results of our actions in the real world. We developed a sense of ownership of our lives, our process, our program, and our world. The feeling of ownership enabled us to become more empowered in our lives.

We are pleased to document the current level of this progressive learning experience in the writings that follows. You will see that commitment, goal setting, and planning created the framework for this educational experience. You also will see that an educational program, which opens the door to the world and invites its students to explore, invariably leads its members to a wealth of unexpected and exciting adventures. We invite you to enjoy the accounts of our adventures with us, as we travel halfway around the world on *a journey to the heart*.

The Learning Community
1989-90 School Year

a journey to the heart

CHAPTER 1: PREPARING FOR THE JOURNEY

**Seeding the idea
Jonathan
Tourzan**

Service has always been a major emphasis of the Learning Community. The 1988-89 Learning Community was no exception. Our group chose to support a service project in Kenya. We raised nearly $2000 to fund a water project in Amakura, a small village in western Kenya. The money supplied the building materials so that the villagers could build a water system for their village.

In Amakura, the women were spending six hours a day in search of water. Our water project brought running water to their village. This, in turn, freed-up large amounts of time, enabling the women to work on improving the quality of life in their village. They used this time to provide education and to improve health care.

The project was funded through IDEX, a San Francisco based development organization. IDEX serves as a broker between Third World country needs and First World funding sources. Our group raised the money to fund the project, and IDEX, in return, provided several opportunities for us to learn about Kenya throughout the school year. They provided us with speakers, such as Alba d'Soza, a native Kenyan and a graduate student in education at Stanford. She talked to our group about economic problems facing Kenya, the role of the government, and the potential benefits of our project. Alba spoke proudly of her homeland and encouraged us to visit someday. This was the first time that we had thought of traveling to Kenya.

In March, IDEX set up a visit with another Kenyan, Daniel Mwayaya. Daniel was traveling in the United States as a guest of World Neighbors, another development agency active in Kenya. Daniel worked as a community organizer in Kenya, traveling from village to village, helping people plan and carry out projects. IDEX had arranged for him to come to our class to give us more background on Third World development.

Daniel showed us pictures of his family and urged us to "come see our fine country." Our students seemed genuinely interested, so Gary, our teacher and program coordinator, asked us if we wanted to go to Kenya during the next school year. All the returning members of our group agreed that this would be a wonderful experience, one to which they were willing to commit. Gary asked Daniel if a visit as short as two weeks would be worth our while. He replied that this amount of time would be sufficient. We could spend one week doing service projects and spend the rest of the time exploring his beautiful country. This idea was beginning to sound very appealing.

Everyone realized that the group would have to be fully committed to realize such a huge task. We set aside time to talk about the possibility of our going. Everyone agreed that it was a great idea. After making sure that our returning students were committed, we informed all incoming students that a trip to Kenya would be part of our experience in the coming year. I would be among those students who would return.

In June, we assembled our incoming group to talk about the trip. At the meeting, summer committees were created to raise funds and make plans. A core group was set up to research grants, to raise funds, and to investigate air fare. We agreed to keep in contact and to update our progress periodically with newsletters.

September 1989: I know that our trip to Kenya will be time-consuming and anxiety-producing; I also know that it will be incredible. As I look ahead, many things come to mind.

Anticipating the lessons
Fiona Hollins

I hope that the itinerary we plan will involve service projects, learning about people, and living with native Kenyans. I bet we will have much to learn from the native people. We also might do some sight-seeing, camping, or teaching. We will encounter difficulties with travel and housing, but I hope our excitement and energy will prevail. We will return to Los Altos with many memories, thoughts, stories, and new attitudes about Africa. We will feel a tremendous sense of accomplishment after the trip and come home with a better understanding of our diverse world.

Before leaving, I had many questions, particularly about the week we would spend working in a village. Would we be welcome? Was there room for us? Would we seem arrogant, idealistic, or foolish? Do the Kenyans have hotels in small poor villages? Would I have to spend a week or two weeks without a shower or real bed? Would I feel like a hypocrite if I didn't go?

Thinking ahead
Andrew Lipson

The week of touring seemed simple enough. An occasional stray bullet from the poachers I can handle, no problem. The plane ride should be terrific — I love planes — and I hope that our flight leaves at 6:30 A.M. so that we can sneak off to the airport while everyone is asleep and catch the rising sun. I can just see us trying to get some businessman from Albuquerque to join in a sing-along.

Once we arrive there, I have no idea how it will be, or what we will learn, or if it will be worth all the effort we put into it. Maybe we'll learn that, "The world isn't so big after all," or that, "People are all truly the same," or that, "I hate poison oak." The experience will be what we make it.

We will have to start preparing now to find out what kind of work we need to do and if we want to do it. Perhaps there are students our age there whom we can visit. Will we be able to understand their accents? How we prepare is as important as the actual trip. I think we should keep track of our goals and see whether we fell short or exceed them.

Debating the issue
Jonathan Tourzan

When the fall term began, we awakened to reality. Six students had withdrawn from the group over the summer, and little work had been done. We were back at stage one, questioning whether the trip would be a possibility. Gary suggested that, even though we had already committed to go, we start at the beginning and decide whether our group was, indeed, committed to go. We agreed and ended up debating this issue for three days. At one point only three students wanted to go. Gradually, the group moved toward a decision.

Making the big decision
Ann Kaye

We spent close to three days trying to reach consensus. At one point, we discovered that twenty-five students were undecided. There were many mixed and unresolved feelings. We decided to declare our positions. Some students said that they would not go unless everyone went. Others said they would go no matter who went, and the remaining few were uncertain about the trip. I was one of the people who did not want to go.

We chose to symbolize our positions by standing, sitting on chairs, or sitting on the floor so that we would have a visual representation of our group. It looked strange to see students positioned on the circle in this way. Those standing wanted to go; those sitting on chairs were undecided; those sitting on the floor did not want to go.

The year seemed to be going by so quickly, and we knew a decision needed to be made soon. Also, fund raising was behind schedule, and the planned departure was only four months away. One by one the students worked through their fears of flying, of getting shots, of failing, and of the unknown. Finally, a decision was made. Every member of our group agreed; all of us would be going to Kenya!

The beginning of this school year started with an intense discussion about whether we should go to Kenya. I did not think the people in the class understood how much work would be involved in setting up the trip. I was hesitant to get involved in such a big project with a group of people who I thought might not work hard enough. I also worried about my own commitment.

All the discussions that we had about going gave us a good push toward working hard. They helped us realize that planning and preparing would not be easy and that it was up to us to do it. I began to feel my own commitment level rise.

Facing the decision
Ryan Marton

At the beginning of the school year, Gary shared a metaphor with us in which he compared our working together in The Learning Community to a group of mountain climbers ascending a mountain. He emphasized that each step of the climb was important, and that we needed to work together to ensure that everyone made it to the top.

In creating our journey to Kenya, we applied the image of a mountain climb to our group's goal of getting everyone to Kenya. We committed ourselves to the basic idea inherent in this imagery, supporting one another and helping each other up the mountain. This concept helped me when things got difficult. The mountain metaphor enabled me to keep my eye on the real goal.

When our group had decided to take on the Kenya adventure, I began looking for ways to further understand the value of the trip by working with the mountain image. Every step we completed in preparing for the trip became another step up the mountain. I saw that every step was a learning experience and valuable to me, even if we did not reach the top. When we completed our task and looked back at the path we had taken, I knew that the experience gained along the way was worth every step.

Imaging a mountain
Jesse Baumgartner

Preparing to climb
Jonathan Tourzan

At this point there was much work to do and not much time to do it. We made a timeline for all the jobs that needed to be done. We set up a subgroup, the *Sherpas*, to track our progress. *Sherpas* are Himalayans who carry loads for mountain expeditions; we liked the symbolism. The work got under way, and we started to move forward.

It was at this point that we received what one of our students, Kelly, called "a gift from God." World Neighbors had brought in a group of farmers from the Philippines who were visiting the U.S. on their way to Honduras. There, they would share agricultural techniques with another community farming project set up by World Neighbors. We told one of the hosts that we were planning to go to Kenya. Her eyes lighted up as she suggested that we talk to Sandra Mardigian, a woman from our area with many ties to Kenya. Sandra had been to Kenya several times for travel and service work, and she knew many people there. After a few phone calls, we had found the woman who profoundly enriched our trip.

Inspiring the group
Fiona Hollins

Gary came to class one day with hundreds of ideas for our trip written in tiny print in his day planner book. He had just returned from a visit with Sandra. She gave us many ideas and possibilities for our trip, which we discussed with great interest.

A week later Sandra brought her Kenyan friend, David Maina, into our classroom. He was a language instructor in Kenya and this was his first trip outside his country. Maina came to share his knowledge of Kenya and its culture with us.

Maina and Sandra brought a wealth of ideas to us for activities while in Kenya. They gave us concrete activities such as *Kiswahili* lessons, rural and urban homestays, and an expedition to Outward Bound Mountain School. Maina was willing to set up homestays for us with his tribal relatives in the country and his friends in the city.

This was the first time that I had met a person from Kenya. The first thing I noticed about Maina was his smile. His grinning presence brightened up the room. When our group greeted him in chorus with, "*Jambo* Maina" (Hello Maina), his whole face glowed. During his morning with us, he shared stories about his family and his home land. He made Kenya come alive for me with vivid descriptions of the country-side and funny stories about his friends.

Photo: Gary Bacon

Prior to his talk with us, our trip to Africa was just an idea, and the places we were going to visit were just names on a map. Now, with Maina beaming at us and telling us how we would love his country, Kenya became *real* for me. I got so excited to go to Africa that I couldn't sit still.

Assuring our safety
Heather Hoppas

While preparing for our trip, many people, especially our parents, expressed concern about our group's health and safety. Concerns ranged from food and water purity to disease prevention and medical treatment. We had several presentations from people who had traveled to Kenya including a physician and other health care professionals. It became clear that we would need to be immunized and take medication with us.

We were fortunate that Laura's mom, Joyce, was accompanying us as a chaperon. Joyce, a registered nurse and a great mom, proved to be a tremendous resource for us. She arranged for us to go as a group to her clinic so that she could give us the required shots. Aside from the considerable expenses that she spared us, getting shots as a group helped reduce the anxiety. Joyce also helped us combine the various forms of health advice that we had received into one comprehensive list. Knowing that everyone had taken the health advice seriously, we were prepared for a safe trip to Kenya.

Accepting the challenge
Jonathan Tourzan

During this time we had begun the arduous task of fund raising. The trip itself would cost almost $60,000, and our family pledges would cover about $30,000. We had already decided that fund raising would be carried out as a group endeavor; consequently, even students who pledged the full $2500 would be committed to help raise money. We decided that each student would raise at least $500 through the Peace Wreath project, and their total contribution would have to equal or exceed $1700, the cost of the air fare. Thus, a person who pledged $1000 would need to raise at least $700. We hoped that the remaining $20,000 would come through grants.

We decided that the next important step would be to create a handbook to describe our trip. The handbook would cover our goals and objectives, itinerary, time line, and fund raising plan. After two weeks of intense labor, including late night computer sessions with Gary, we completed the handbook. We felt very proud of it; we knew that it would give us a strong base from which to develop our journey.

The Peace Wreath project worked in an interesting way. We would ask people to support our trip by writing a message of goodwill on a ribbon. The rainbow of ribbons would then be tied to four wreaths. These would be given to groups of Kenyans with whom we would be staying during our trip. The wreaths were symbolic of the love and goodwill that our donors were extending to the people of Kenya. Everyone who supported us would be, in a sense, coming with us. It was a beautiful idea.

On November ninth we inaugurated the project. At first it went slowly. Finally a few students starting bringing in donations. Then things started to move. Author Ron Jones, who works for the Recreation Center for the Handicapped in San

Francisco, helped us in two ways. He wrote his professional colleagues inviting them to join in our Wreath Project, and he performed an evening of story telling for the public that brought in substantial support. Jesse received a $1000 donation. Over the next ten consecutive days our group collected $1000 each day. By the time our first deadline came, we had demonstrated our ability to raise large sums of money. After a group recommitment, we decided to extend the deadline and keep going with the Peace Wreath.

"Ding! Dong!" chimed the doorbell. I paused, listening for a reply. "Hello, who's there?" a voice inside the house finally answered.

Dealing with resistance
Andrew Lipson

"Hello, my name is Andy Lipson, and I'm a student of the Learning Community at Los Altos High School," I said quickly. A woman opened the door and looked out at me. I went on, not giving her a chance to tell me to go away, "This February we're taking a trip to Kenya as part of a cultural exchange. We'll be staying there for about three weeks. While we're there we'll be staying with families in Nairobi and in a rural area. Umm, we'll also be doing service projects."

I felt unsure, worried that I was imposing. I hardly stopped to take a breath, "Uhh, to make sure all our students can afford to go, we're doing fund raisers and, umm, the one that I have here today is the Peace Wreath, and you write a message on this ribbon, and then we'll take all the ribbons and put them on a wreath. We will then take it with us to Kenya to give to the people we meet there. We're looking for donations of twenty-five dollars but anything, more or less, is greatly appreciated."

I was lucky if I got that far. Most of the time people were not even home. When they were, I would give the whole speech in one quick breath with adrenalin coursing through my body. The responses would vary greatly. Usually they would just give me a stock answer.

"Well, it sounds interesting, but ..."

"I'm sorry, I have three children in college right now and ..."

"I'm not interested."

"Why don't you earn the money yourself?"

Usually, if I went to twenty houses in which people were home, I would get at least one who would give me a donation. Through all my efforts, I received about sixty donations. I had saved some money from my summer job, and my parents each made contributions. I still would not have been able to go without the financial help of the group. Fortunately, some of my classmates had raised more than they needed, and they were willing to share with me.

I hated asking people for money; it made me so vulnerable. We each committed to a fund raising goal; then we had *check-ins* each morning to make sure that everyone was following through. Many students found it difficult to keep up the pace or to deal with so much rejection. We had long talks about commitments, and we would give encouragement to the people who were having trouble.

My main problem me was that every time I reached one goal and conquered it, there always seemed to be another bug-eyed razor-toothed goal just waiting for me. It was not easy for me to go out and raise money, but I did it, and I learned how to extend myself and go beyond my personal comfort zones.

Assembling the messages
Jenelle Flaherty

We went door-to-door for three months talking to people about our goals for Kenya and what we hoped to experience. We asked for donations ranging from five dollars to one thousand dollars.

I felt uncomfortable every time I walked up to a door collecting money. I continued going around talking with people because I knew this trip would be very valuable to me, and I wanted to include my community in my experience.

I walked up to a door on Marich Way in Los Altos and rang the doorbell. I was not feeling good about going door-to-door right then; I had not gotten a donation all afternoon. A man answered the door with a smile. I explained our goals for the trip and told him that I would really appreciate a small donation. I was very excited as he went back in his house and came out with a check for fifty dollars!

I regained my enthusiasm immediately. In exchange for the money that this generous man donated, I handed him a ribbon on which to write a message. He wrote, "May our community bring friendship to your community." Other people wrote about friendship, love, and peace. Other donors wrote things like, "May peace guide your way" and "Save the elephants." Some people just signed it. All of these responses were invaluable to our trip because they involved the donor in the our purpose.

We began to meet our financial goals while collecting from our community over seven hundred pastel ribbons in all colors of the rainbow. We bought four wreaths made of intertwined grape vines. We completed our Peace Wreaths by tying the ribbons around the edges of the vines. The finished products were four beautiful Peace Wreaths that symbolized our community's love and friendship.

During this period, four students decided not to go on the trip. Two left the program at the semester while the other two, Adam and Ann, stayed on. Losing some of our members was disappointing to the group. Now we realized that not everyone would be going, but no change was made in our decision to go. Our commitment level remained high.

Losing some members

Jonathan Tourzan

The Peace Wreath Project was challenging, strenuous, and fun. My experience while going door-to-door was great. I met people who really understood and appreciated our group goals for Kenya.

Supporting the group

Ann Kaye

We had worked hard to formulate our goals for our Kenya trip. We wanted to develop an understanding of the people, to learn about the country's social and ecological issues, and, above all, to contribute to the creation of a better world.

I also encountered some people who did not understand the significance of our trip. I learned slowly how to accept rejections and how to take in negative comments. At first, it was discouraging, but, as I continued, the strength of our purpose seemed to overshadow those feelings.

I collected donations for the trip although I had reneged on my commitment to go. Many students expressed concern about why I chose not to go. My answer would be, "I don't know," or "I just don't want to go," followed with a brief and simple explanation of my choice. Usually, I would feel that my choice was too personal to explain. When I collected money for the Peace Wreath project, I would tell people that, although I was not going with my class, I was out there supporting them. It was strange explaining a trip that I was not taking. Yet, because of the feeling I got from my fund raising efforts, I became more certain that I wanted to continue to be a contributing member of the group.

Meeting the goal
Jonathan
Tourzan

The extended deadline allowed more students to fulfill their fund raising commitments. Each day when our group met, we checked to see how much money had been raised. We encouraged the people having difficulty to keep up the effort. The weeks seemed like months during this intense fund raising, but we met our goal. By winter vacation, we had over two thirds of the trip fund raised; it was clear that the trip would be a reality.

Although several large donations came in over winter vacation, we realized that we would not receive large institutional grants. When we came back to school, we decided to push on with the Peace Wreath Project because people supported the concept. This meant more door-to-door collection, more check-ins, and more tension. Most students committed to raise another $500, and some raised even more.

Gaining
confidence
Katy Arnovick

Going door-to-door was a major activity for me. It was one of the most difficult activities I ever had to do. First, I had to learn to present myself; then I had to learn how to explain the project. The hard thing about this was that I had to be brief yet gain their attention, convincing them to donate. On top of that, I had to motivate myself to go out and try to raise money. To do this, I had to set my attitude and go out with enthusiasm.

I finally got comfortable with my speech, and people started donating money. Then I went to a house where the lady said that she thought what I was doing was horrible. She said that I should find another way to collect money for our trip, instead of bothering people in their homes. This was the first person who had been negative. I got so discouraged that I lost my motivation. I was not sure how to take what she said. I almost cried and kept thinking that I was bothering people. "Maybe all the people that gave me money just gave it to me so that I would leave them alone," I thought.

I decided to talk to Julie and see how she was doing. I found out that she had had a similar experience, and we came to the conclusion that going out together might help us to be more confident. We went out the next day with a new attitude about raising money. We realized that *we were giving people an opportunity to join us in a worthwhile project*. We became very successful together. I found it very helpful to have someone there for support if I became discouraged.

Throughout the experience of going door-to-door, I learned about my motivation and my ability to commit myself one hundred percent. This activity has been very significant in my life. I feel that it will serve me in future activities that require me to speak with conviction to individuals or groups.

By the end of the semester, we had raised all the money, and our itinerary was set. We knew that in a few weeks we would be in Kenya. At the beginning of the new semester, three more students enrolled in our program. They decided that they wanted to go to Kenya with us. Their families pledged, and we received another large donation which enabled them to join us. Estill Travel succeeded in adding three more tickets to our reservation; it seemed that nothing could stop us now. We would be taking twenty-one students to Kenya.

Readying for lift-off
Jonathan Tourzan

The last few weeks before our trip were hectic. We had to get immunizations, to decide what to bring, to assemble the Peace Wreaths, and to do all the little things that need to be done before taking a long trip.

Before we left, we had a *bon voyage*, potluck dinner with our parents to celebrate our success. After dinner, Sandra, who had just returned from Kenya, reviewed the details of our itinerary for the parents. Then Gary gave each student a special gift, an implement used in climbing. We received carabiners, pitons, wedges, sling webbing, and pieces of colorful rope to symbolize that we had climbed our metaphorical mountain in organizing our trip. We could not believe that in a few days we would be flying to Kenya.

When we arrived at the San Francisco Airport, we were all filled with an amazing feeling of accomplishment. We had come so far from those talks with Alba and Daniel. We had made a dream into a reality and we were about to embark on the experience of a lifetime. As the plane lifted off the runway, a whole new adventure began.

CHAPTER 2: EXPLORING THE INNER CITY

After a twenty hour flight and a nine hour lay-over in London, we landed in Nairobi, Kenya. It was Thursday morning, February 16, 1990. Walking off the airplane, we got our first look at Kenya. The land was a flat, grassy savannah which seemed to stretch endlessly to the horizon. Acacia trees dotted the landscape. As I looked around at the terrain, I was reminded of nature shows that I had watched back home.

Arriving in Kenya

Jon Rinard

The hot, humid air greeted us as we walked off the plane and stayed with us until we entered customs. After having my passports stamped, I waited for my classmates; I noticed that everyone passing by looked so dressed up. Most of the men were wearing slacks, a dress shirt, and a sport coat. "Gosh," I thought, "how can they do that? It must be at least eighty-five degrees."

I didn't fully comprehend that we were on the other side of the world until Jonathan exclaimed: "Can you believe it? We're in Kenya you guys!" Then I *could* believe it. It seemed as if my heart stopped for a second. Other than London, I had never been outside the U.S.. For the next eighteen days, I would have some of the most memorable experiences of my life.

**Jumping right in
Jonathan
Tourzan**

We had arrived! We walked across the runway, through immigration, and straight to the baggage claim. All around us were signs in both *Kiswahili*, the national language of Kenya, and English. We had fun trying to pronounce these words correctly and discover their meanings.

After we had all passed through customs, we pulled our group together and acknowledged the moment; we had arrived safely in Kenya. Gary gave everyone four hundred Kenyan shillings—about twenty dollars in U.S. currency—so that we would have some spending money. Then we walked out of the airport. Our Kenyan host, David Maina, was waiting there with three vans. "*Karibuni Kenya!*" (Welcome to Kenya!), he exclaimed. After several handshakes and friendly greetings, we put our baggage into the vans and sped off to the Nairobi Game Park.

We got our first taste of Kenyan wildlife at the gate of the game park. There was a colorful tree, teeming with hundreds of birds. These birds would dart in and out of small nests into the sky. I had never seen anything like it.

**Weaving
memories
Joyce Zarcone**

One of the most colorful and melodic memory I have of Kenya is of the Weaver Birds. The female bird weaves herself into her nest to sit upon her eggs until they hatch. These birds are bright yellow with black markings and have a lovely song. We saw them in many places, but the largest number were in a thorny Acacia tree at the entrance to the Nairobi Game Park on our first morning in Kenya. What a spectacular welcome!

The game park, like most of the Nairobi area, was flat to the horizon. Dry grass covered the land, and an occasional tree could be seen reaching up into the sky. The game park consisted of pristine land with small dirt roads cut through for *safari* vans. These roads were bumpy and, being tall, I hit the roof of the van several times. While driving along the dirt trails of the game park, we saw a jackal, warthogs, gazelles, ostrich, hartebeests, and lions. I was struck by the sheer laziness of the lions. After their early morning hunt, they seemed completely uninterested in our presence. They did not even move when our vans drove up to them.

After this excursion, we drove a few miles to Nairobi. The girls were taken to the YWCA, the boys to the YMCA. We had not known that we were to have separate accommodations, and this change caused some anxiety. We put our baggage into our rooms and cleaned up. There was no food at the YWCA, so the girls went to a little restaurant where we joined them for lunch. Maina was there, and he elaborated on our itinerary. We still were not sure what to expect. We discovered right away, however, how far our money would go. For forty shillings, about two dollars, we could get enough food to feed two people, which was inexpensive by our standards.

Later that afternoon we had an introductory *Kiswahili* lesson. Maina taught us some helpful phrases for the city. After the lesson we walked together across the *Uhuru* (Freedom) Highway to the market. This is one of the main streets in Nairobi and is right behind the YMCA. Because we were near the university, the streets were bustling with students. We found Nairobi to be a city of opposites. There were large skyscrapers right next to old, run-down buildings, and men in business suits walking next to beggars. Small shops and restaurants lined the busy streets. I found Nairobi with its sharp contrasts and busy life unlike anywhere I had ever been.

Adjusting to the city
Jonathan Tourzan

When we arrived at the YMCA, Maina introduced us to Julius. Julius is an instructor at Maina's language school in Nairobi. They both became our instant friends and companions.

Meeting Julius
Megan Mathias

Photos: Gary Bacon

Julius' tribal home, Kitu, is a large town east of Nairobi in Kamba territory. He spent the early part of his life there, but, as there are few jobs in his rural district, he came to Nairobi several years ago to find work.

What I remember best about Julius was his friendly smile. I loved how he said, "My name is Julius," with his rich tribal accent. When teaching *Kiswahili* his smile would always come through. Whenever we answered a question correctly, he would smile and raise his finger and say, "*Ndio*" (yes, that is correct).

When I spoke with him, he was always pleasant and very easy to get to know. He wanted to know all that he could about America; this desire made for active conversations. Since I have returned, my memory of his smile remains vivid.

When we first arrived in Kenya, I wanted to meet someone and talk to them, using the *Kiswahili* that I had learned at school before we left. During the drive from the airport to the YWCA, I hung out the window of the van and called out, *"Jambo!"* (Hello!) to everyone I saw. I was excited when they understood me and waved back.

When I got to the YWCA, a 20 year old Kenyan girl named Juliette came into my room looking for my roommate. She was my next door neighbor, but she always hung out in my room. When she saw me, she ran over and shook my hand. I took the opportunity to practice my *Kiswahili* again and said, *"Habari gani?"* (How are you?). She responded, *"Nzuri!"* (Good!), and we both started laughing.

**Greeting people
Julie Paiva**

When I walked up to the front desk of the YWCA, I was struck by the women who were working there. They were very friendly, but they worked slowly, so it took quite a while for me to get the key to my room. Their calm manner, however, created a very relaxed ambiance.

I walked down the stone path in the garden that led to my room. I took in the beauty of the tall, green trees and the exotic flowers, each with unique colors. The warm air and sunshine felt good on my skin.

I found my room where I met my roommate, Jayne-Rose; she was the best! After her friend had come over to borrow a blouse, we talked about borrowing and lending things. Jayne told me: "My friends feel bad asking me for things because they don't want me to think they're using me."

Her face took on a more serious look as she exclaimed: "But no! I love to give. If I have something, and I don't need it, I will give." She thought for a moment and continued; "The other day someone stole the room key from the front desk and came and stole all the money that I had in my room. But, you know, if she was that desperate for money, it's okay. I think God might have meant it to be that way."

Her inner and outer beauty touched me. I liked the way she thought. She always put others before herself. I was excited to have such a beautiful person for a roommate.

**Making friends
Kelly McJunkin**

Changing standards
Ryan Marton

When I first arrived in Nairobi it was hard for me to get used to the living conditions at the YMCA. I was uncomfortable with everything including the bedrooms, the bathrooms, and the people. I did not like being crowded in a room with five other people. I also felt uncomfortable with the strange insects that I saw and the mosquitoes that buzzed my head at night when I tried to sleep.

The accommodations were so simple compared to my home in Los Altos Hills; they felt dirty and cheap to me. The food in the dining hall look so strange that I didn't want to eat. I was afraid that I was going to starve.

As time and the scent of soap on my body passed, I began to get used to everything; my standards were changing. I saw how some people had to live in Nairobi, and I even began to see the benefits of the YMCA. As I gradually got used to my surroundings, I began to appreciate what I had. I thought that the YMCA was like a palace with gourmet food. Most importantly, I discovered that I didn't need as much as I thought I needed in order to be comfortable.

Reading the ribbons
Kelly McJunkin

We had overcome our most difficult task in raising over $60,000 for our trip. We had almost given up at times, but, in the end, we always persisted. While knocking on doors in Los Altos, Mountain View, and Palo Alto, I had to remind myself that there is an abundance of love and compassion in our community. Finding it was the hard part, but we succeeded. We were able to represent the love and support of our community in the 750 pastel ribbons tied to 4 woven wicker wreaths. Now this rainbow of ribbons had traveled around the world to Kenya, connecting our two countries with love.

Jayne, my roommate at the YWCA, smiled joyfully as she read the messages on the ribbons from the wreath that I had carried to Kenya. I explained to her that the wreath would be given to select groups on our trip. She was saddened not to be one of them; she found the wreath so beautiful.

As I looked at the wreath, I could see beyond our hard work. I also saw the essence behind the Peace Wreath. We had carried messages of peace, love, and unity from our country to Kenya. The Kenyans found the messages to be so important; they readily opened their hearts to accept them. The messages reinforced the idea that we are all one people hoping to find peace in our lives.

After a short walk through downtown Nairobi, we arrived at the market. The market was a busy two story building packed with people. Vendors were selling fruit and vegetables, and souvenirs, such as woodwork, baskets, and jewelry. There was even a meat market in the back, but this was for locals more than for tourists. The vendors in the market were aggressive. One vendor coaxed me into buying a pineapple for which, it turned out, I paid an exorbitant price. Many beggars who hung around the marketplace approached us and asked for shillings.

Walking to market
Jonathan Tourzan

After some free time to explore the market, we walked to a shop where we bought postcards to send to our Peace Wreath donors. The storekeepers were shocked when they discovered that we wished to purchase 750 postcards, far more than the typical sale. We sent these postcards to all the generous people in the U.S. who had written messages on our ribbons and had donated money to our trip.

On my second day in Nairobi, I walked into the Nairobi marketplace without knowing what to expect. The smells of people, fresh produce, and wood products swirled in the air. Dust billowed up in clouds around my feet as merchants and buyers bustled around me. As I walked deeper into this commotion, peddlers kept stopping me, trying to sell their bracelets to me. I felt overwhelmed and found that the only way I could maintain my composure was to keep my eyes on the ground and say, "No!" to everyone who approached me.

Feeling overwhelmed
Rebecca Sugg

Each seller tried to get my attention by showing me his wares and insisting that his were better than his competitors. I spent several minutes walking around, trying to adapt to the overwhelming chaos of the market. I became too confused to buy anything and I left in a daze.

After I left the market, I walked around to a side street to meet the rest of the group. As I turned the corner, I noticed my classmates besieged by small children asking for Kenyan shillings. I drew a little closer, amused by my classmates' confused and distraught faces.

Suddenly, I was hit by a crowd of what seemed like flying torpedoes. Small arms wrapped around me like clamps. I regained my balance and looked down and saw a small, dark face with pleading eyes looking up at me. I couldn't resist and handed the little girl two shillings. I hoped that this would satisfy her and that she would be on her way, yet it only encouraged her. She would not let go; I had to pry her hands off my arm. I began to get angry as more children surrounded me asking for money. I gave Ryan a sharp annoyed look for directing the children my way. Finally, when the children realized that I had given all my spare change away, they scurried off. After all of this, I was looking forward to leaving this chaotic place.

Expanding our view
Jonathan Tourzan

That evening, we ate dinner at the YMCA and discussed our first impressions of Nairobi. We still could hardly believe that we were in Kenya. Afterward, Maina and Julius gave us a brief *Kiswahili* lesson, teaching us some simple greetings in *Kiswahili*. The long flight and busy first day activities had exhausted us, however, so shortly, we returned to our rooms and called it a day.

The next morning we were awakened by the busy sounds and fresh smells of Nairobi. After a cold shower and a breakfast at the YMCA, we were ready to start our first full day in Kenya. The YMCA proved to be an interesting accommodation. It had a swimming pool and a snack bar, making it a popular hang out for students. It was also the place where tourists of limited means, such as young Africans and Europeans, stayed while in Nairobi. People would gather on the large open porch in the afternoon looking for company, and small groups of adventuresome travelers swapped exciting stories with each other. People were friendly and easy to engage in conversation.

That morning Julius and Maina taught our group more useful *Kiswahili* phrases in preparation for our urban and rural homestays. We learned how to tell time in Kenya. We would say, "*Ni saa ngapi?*" (How many hours are there?). The response was, "*Ni saa nbili ya asubuhi*," (There are two hours this morning). In Kenya, however, the day starts at 6 A.M. when the sun rises and ends at 6 P.M. when the sun sets. So two hours in the morning refers to 8:00 A.M. Likewise, six hours in the night refers to 12:00 midnight. This system works because Kenya is on the equator, and the sun rises and sets at almost the same time throughout the year.

Later that morning we met David Ferris, a University of California exchange student at Nairobi University. David and his Kenyan friend, Isabelle, gave us a tour of the university and talked to us about education in Kenya. He explained that the school emphasizes memorization rather than understanding. He also explained that the government actively controls what is taught and what is discussed among the students, even in informal discussions. I thought that this kind of government intrusion into the life of a university student, coupled with the required three month tour of duty in the Army that each student must complete, produced a repressive atmosphere on the university campus.

David then took us to his room in a university dormitory. It was very small and had one bed and a small desk. He explained that most students share a small room, yet he had been lucky enough to receive a single room. All the dormitories had common bathrooms and recreation rooms. Afterward, Isabelle took us to the women's dormitory. Her room was considerably larger than David's. After our tour we said good-bye to David and Isabelle and returned to the YMCA for lunch. We had discovered many striking differences between education in Kenya and America, differences that made me appreciate the opportunities that I have.

I am a city person. I love cities, especially cities with character. When I first set my eyes on Nairobi, I fell in love instantly. People packed the streets. I watched men and women carrying large sacks on their heads. Small groups of high-spirited

Reflecting a smile
Vanessa Tubbs

school children, some walking barefoot, scurried about. Cab drivers were tearing around corners, almost crashing into people and cars. Tons of chocolate colored people were going about their daily doings.

There I stood in awe. "What a great place to be," I thought. As I stood there, I didn't realize that I had a silly smile on my face until I saw my reflection in a store window. To my surprise, I noticed an old man staring back at me through the window. He smiled and yelled, "*Jambo!*" I yelled back, "*Jambo!*" Then I felt that same silly smile coming back on my face.

Saving my shillings
Ian Perkins

As we approached our first market in Nairobi, men with shiny, wooden animal necklaces ran up to me and to the other members of the group. One man put a necklace on me and said: "Because I am poor, you will buy two necklaces from me for two hundred shillings."

I put the necklaces back on him and said: "You have to wake up early in the morning to pull one over on me."

Meeting Father Grol
Jonathan Tourzan

That evening we were ready to visit the *Undugu* (Brotherhood) Society. This organization was founded by a Catholic priest, Father Grol, who had been a missionary in Kenya for over thirty years. In his younger days, Father Grol traveled from village to village, either on foot or by donkey, to serve the people.

When he tired of traveling, he chose to spread the Christian gospel of love by starting an organization to provide education and job training to street children. The organization became the *Undugu* Society. It offered housing to any boy who would promise to stay off drugs. Father Grol hoped that the opportunities provided by his society would give homeless children a chance to become productive citizens.

A large bus picked us up at two hours in the evening (8:00 P.M.) to take us to the home of the *Undugu* Boys. It took us through downtown Nairobi into the Mathare Valley, the poorest section of Nairobi. Here we traveled on rough roads, passing shanties and roadside vendors. We were on our way to Father Grol's Undugu Boys' Home.

We arrived at a small compound where about 35 young boys greeted our group. They were shy at first and said very little to us. The tall, older white man among them, Father Grol, welcomed us and took us into a small colorful room with mural lined walls.

The rooms were too small to accommodate everyone, so the Undugu Boys and our students stood in separate rooms and could see each other through an open doorway. The light was dim, and it was hard to see everyone's faces. Three boys with smiles that lighted up the room stepped up and began to sing a welcome song. We couldn't help but join in when we knew the words.

Being the world
Kelly McJunkin

Photo: Kelly McJunkin

Samuel, who had the brightest smile of all, began strumming the chords to *We Are the World* on his guitar; he asked us if we knew the words. The excitement and laughter spread as we began to sing the words together.

"We are the world,

We are the children,

We are the ones

    who make a brighter day,

So let's start giving."

As we sang, I cried inner tears of joy; I felt united with these people who live on the other side of my world. The truth rang out in the song that we are the children, and our generation can change the future of the world. The connection that we felt in that small room made it seem as if the whole world was sharing our joy. Putting our cultural differences aside, we danced and laughed and smiled. It was a great way to start our trek through Kenya.

Singing for peace
Joyce Zarcone

We continued to sing for and with each other. The Kenyans sang songs in *Kiswahili* — *Malaika* and *Jambo* — and in English — *Leaving on a Jet Plane*, *The Boxer*, and *Kingston Town*. The communication grew between the two groups as we all sang *Malaika* (*My Angel*), a Kenyan song that we had learned back home. That evening, a picture of hope for one world brought tears to my eyes and a lump to my throat.

Then our students gave a special presentation. We had brought two soccer balls, thirty pair of soccer shoes, two pair of boxing gloves, and clothing from America to give to the Undugu Boys. Each of us had carried a new pair of soccer shoes in our packs, which made this exchange feel more personal. The Undugu Boys' eyes lighted up when they saw the gifts. Afterwards, we posed for a group picture and danced together. The world seemed like a very small place that evening with its people having so much in common.

Sparring to music
Jonathan Tourzan

Soccer is one of the most popular sports in Kenya since one needs very little equipment to play. Father Grol was hoping to field two soccer teams, and our gifts made this possible.

Also, the new boxing gloves, which Sandra and her friend Doug had sent with us, ensured that more boys would be able to practice the sport.

Father Grol sees many benefits in boxing. He believes that it is a healthy release for all his boys and even a way out of poverty for some. He organizes boxing leagues within the city, often without the full approval of the hierarchy of the Church.

The boys put on their new boxing gloves and gave us a show as they sparred for a few short rounds. The other boys gathered around the boxers and hummed a beautiful, hypnotic song. Their singing produced a magical quality in the room that made the whole experience surrealistic.

The rhythmic beat of the song coupled with the graceful movements of the boxers fused my awareness into a group consciousness. The duality of observer and observed had become transparent.

Eating and dancing
Fiona Hollins

The Undugu boys brought out a generous feast of *chapati* (fried bread), beans, cabbage, and meat stew. "We made the dinner ourselves," they told me proudly and brought us water to wash our hands before eating. Fortunately, Father Grol started by scooping up a chapati full of food so that we would know how to eat the meal without plates or silverware.

This was our first real Kenyan meal. Here we were in the middle of the poorest part of Nairobi, eating with street kids, and feeling perfectly comfortable. This became our baptism to Kenyan food; almost all eating was easy after this experience.

After dinner, two Undugu boys played reggae songs on their guitars while the others sang along and danced. I joined a few brave members of our group in the dance. As everyone became less self-conscious, more of our group started dancing together in the dark crowded room. I felt accepted by the Kenyan boys; I knew that we were all the same inside.

When it was time to say good-bye, the boys taught us their special handshake. We slapped hands and touched thumbs. As we joined hands, the idea of a united world seemed entirely possible.

Finding purpose
Heather Hoppas

I felt close to the boys and had a hard time leaving. We grudgingly got back in the buses to return to the YMCA. As we were driving back from the Undugu Boys' Home, I realized why we were in Kenya. We were there to support the people in any way we could and to make friendships that we would always remember. It was at the Boys' Home that I started to interact with Kenyans and learn more about their values and way of life.

Seeing the
culture
Jonathan
Tourzan

The next day was our last in Nairobi before the homestays. Our *Kiswahili* lessons became more intense. Maina also gave us a brief overview of the tribal system in Kenya. We learned that in Kenya there are forty-two tribes that can be grouped into three larger tribal groupings. These are the Bantus, Nilotes, and Coastals whose differentiations are based on ethnic background and language. For example, the Maasai are Nilotic and have a separate ethnic background from Kikuyus or Kambas who are Bantus.

The Coastal tribes have more Arabic blood. Coastal tribes, such as Swahilis, also have a stronger Arabic influence in their languages because of Muslim influences. For example, the word in *Kiswahili* for soldier is *askari*. In Arabic the word is the same. This has special significance to me because my family name is Askari Tourzani, which means *Soldier from Tourzan*. Maina also explained that most people identify strongly with their tribes. All this information was invaluable for our homestays as it gave us a greater understanding of the heritage of the people with whom we would be staying.

After lunch, we went to the Kenyan National Museum. There, we learned more about Kenyan tribal history and lifestyle, and the origins of man. The museum had a fascinating display of tribal jewelry, tools, and instruments. There were drums, lutes, and woodwinds, all traditional Kenyan instruments. Being a bamboo flute player, I was fascinated by the variety of flutes in the display cases. Colorful clothing and jewelry from different tribes also adorned the museum walls. The clothing was divided into age group and tribe. For example, I marveled at a very large and beautiful earring traditionally worn by a childless Kamba wife.

There was also an excellent exhibit on the origins of humanity and subhuman species, such as *Homo erectus*. Included in this exhibit was a large stone painting with wildebeests and gazelles. There were also old tools, such as stone arrows and old bones. Some anthropologists believe that the human species originated in Kenya, and there were duplicates of some very ancient skeletal finds that support this claim. Another interesting possession of the museum was the world's largest elephant. When this elephant was alive, the Kenyan Army protected it from poachers. The museum has preserved its remains for all to admire.

After seeing the museum, we walked to a second market located near an Islamic mosque. This market sold mostly wooden carvings, jewelry, and other miscellaneous souvenirs. We browsed through the market and then got a quick look at the nearby mosque. Unfortunately, we could not enter the mosque because we were not Muslims, but we did get a chance to admire its beautiful architecture. There were several Muslims who made their evening prayers outside the mosque, and I watched with interest.

That night we had a meeting to prepare for our homestays. Maina gave us some clues on what to expect. He answered all our questions and taught us more useful phrases for our homestays. He explained that our hosts would expect us to eat several helpings of food and that they would find it rude if we did not finish our food. If we would say, "*Nimeshiba sana*" (I am very satisfied) and smile nicely, then they would understand that we had eaten enough and would not be offended.

Preparing for homestays
Jonathan Tourzan

We finished the evening by writing messages on the postcards that we were sending to our Peace Wreath sponsors in the U.S.. All the students sent a personal message to everyone from whom they had received a ribbon. After we finished this task, we went to bed curious and excited about what new adventures the next day would bring.

The next day our homestays began. Half of the group took a van from the YMCA to Muranga, while the other half waited at the YMCA for their homestay families. Most students went to Fort Jesus, a Nairobi suburb, on the north side of town. A few students, however, stayed in a south Nairobi suburb. Each student stayed with families of different age and social status.

Each student stayed with their Nairobi family for three days and two nights, and, after the homestays, we returned to the YMCA to discuss our impressions. With Maina's help, we processed some of our experiences. Each student shared his or her unique experience with the group. These insights into the homestay of each student helped to clarify some nebulous thoughts that individual students might have had about their own experience.

Crossing over
Heather Hoppas

My first homestay was in Nairobi. I felt nervous and excited as I waited for my homestay mom to arrive. As she walked toward me, I noticed her beautiful, bright eyes and her small, tight braids. She had a wonderful, warm smile and was wearing a long blue dress. After we greeted each other, we started walking to the market. When we got there, she told me that we were buying food for supper.

As we crossed the street, she held my hand, and I felt relieved because I forgot which way to look before crossing the street. I still had not gotten use to cars driving on the left side of the street in Kenya. After shopping, we stopped in a store for sodas, got on a bus, and headed for my new home.

Jumping in
with my father
Ian Perkins

At the YMCA in Nairobi, I sat on the porch with Jon waiting for my homestay parents to pick me up. It seemed like hours before it was time to go. I saw a nicely dressed man in a business suit. He had a smile that lighted up the room, a smile that went straight to my heart. "I hope he's my father," I said to Jon.

The man walked closer to me and said: "You are Ian, no?" "Yes, I am," I said. He sat next to me and said the magic words: "I am James Muya, your father."

I quickly left the porch to get my bags. When I returned, Jesse, another member of our group, told me that my *father* and his *mother* were siblings. I realized that Jesse was going to be my cousins, and that he would live near me. We all began the thirty minute walk to the bus stop.

I was carrying a heavy backpack, and as I walked to the *matatu* (small bus) that would take us home, the dust from the road got in my eyes. The sun beat on my neck, and I noticed that I was sweating like a pig. I looked at Jesse; he was sweating too. "Man it's hot," I thought. Yet, when I looked at my *father*, he only appeared to be *warm*. "He must be used to it," I marveled.

That night, I slept in my sleeping bag on the couch. The house had only one room, and there was a curtain to divide the living room from the bedroom where James and *Mama* Stella slept. Their two children, Stella and Louie, slept in another part of the compound with the housekeeper.

In the middle of the night, my dad woke me and asked me if I wanted to sleep in their bed with them. I laughed and asked, "Why?" He explained that it was raining, the old roof tiles were leaking, and my sleeping bag was getting wet. In "two shakes of a rabbit's tail," I leaped into their bed. Although I had known my family for less than a full day, I felt like I had known them for years.

Giving heart gifts
Leah Mowery

I got up in the morning from my bed and went outside. I felt warm from the sun, and I could hear the sounds of people out on the dirt road just beyond my family's fence. My sister, Marriane, gave me some water to wash with and a cup to brush my teeth. Because they didn't have running water for the sink or a shower, I went into a dark stall and washed my arms, legs and face. I felt good tucked away in this cool, dark corner, and the water was refreshing.

After I packed, we had breakfast together. Marriane had prepared French toast and cocoa for me. We sat and talked, knowing that this was my last day. I felt good being with her — so connected. The last night we had stayed up and talked for hours. She told me about her home out in the countryside, about how people caught fish there, and about the different beliefs that they followed. One story told of a group of religious people who would go around at night in a trance, trying to scare people by scratching on doors or windows. If they did not succeed, they would go away. She told me that she felt relieved not to live there anymore.

Then she stood up and took a basket from a shelf. "This is a present for you," she said. "It is from Mombasa. I will get you some more when I go there. It is for carrying fruit and vegetables."

I felt so happy. I got out my present for her, a colored scarf; I felt that it was somehow inadequate. It alone couldn't express all the gratitude and happiness that I felt.

As I was leaving, *Mama* Marriane gave me a *kanga* (wrap around skirt) to wear. We stood there together, and I felt like

Photo: Gary Bacon

these people were giving me so much. They provided me with a wonderful experience in their home, and they also showed me appreciation through their gifts.

**Losing a leader
Jonathan
Tourzan**

During the homestays there was much speculation about the death of Mr. Robert Ouko, the Minister of Foreign Affairs. Mr. Ouko had endeared himself to the Kenyan people through his brilliant work in his governmental position. This popular man had been assassinated a few days before our homestays, and there was suspicion among the people that someone in the government was responsible. People were demanding a full explanation of his mysterious death, and the demands brought about demonstrations when no proper explanations were given. People throughout Nairobi were upset by the loss of this great man.

There was great mourning over the brutal slaying of Dr. Ouko, especially by the people of his tribe, the Luos. My host family was Luo. They were very jovial and friendly people by nature, but I could tell that they felt a great loss from this man's death. My host brother, Sammy, told me that he was going to the funeral and asked me if I would like to go with him. I felt it would be a great honor to experience a part of Kenyan history first hand. I wanted to go to the funeral of this admired and respected man. Also, I wanted to be part of the family and do what my brother did. I did not even think that this might be an unwise thing for a foreigner to do.

Walking into a riot
Bruce Epis

The next morning we took a bus to town. After we got off the bus, we walked about four blocks up a hill to the largest church in Nairobi. Upon our arrival, we were surprised to find the church was already full of mourners. Sammy and I joined the large crowd of people gathered outside. Amplifiers were placed outside so the people could hear as the services got under way. I saw men and women crying as they heard the eulogy.

When the service was over, people wanted to pass by the coffin to view the body, but the government officials would not permit it. The people outside reacted by chanting, "We want to see the body!" Sammy suggested that we move behind the crowd of protesters in case we needed to run; we moved quickly to observe from a safer distance.

The chanting persisted which caused the officer in charge to order riot police to move toward the crowd. Some people in the crowd began to run, while others began to throw rocks at the police. The police shot twice to disperse the people, causing everyone to run. I remember hearing tear gas canisters exploding behind me in the distance. While most of the people ran frantically down the hill, Sammy took my hand and ran with me to the entrance of the church grounds next door, but we could not get inside because the gates were locked. Fortunately, some nuns came running out of the church and let a group of us into the grounds. They then locked the gates behind us. Sammy told me that we were safe on the grounds of the church.

I could not believe what had just happened; my heart was pumping very fast, and my legs were shaking. Then my eyes started to burn as tear gas began drifting in. We all hurried into the church to avoid the stinging pain. To my surprise, paramedics brought a lady into the church on a stretcher; she had been hit by a rock in the head. Minutes later four other injured people were brought in on stretchers. One lady was hysterical and kept crying and screaming. I also saw a few militia men walking around talking to each other in the church. Sammy went back outside to see if things had cooled down. He told me that everyone had run away, and we could leave now.

Later that day Sammy told me that violent behavior of this sort was very rare in Kenya. He assured me that people would settle down once the body was flown from Nairobi to the Luo homeland for burial.

After eating lunch downtown, we returned home, and I told the other American students what had happened. They were glad that I was okay, and they helped me realize that I should not have gone to the funeral. I could have gotten hurt or arrested and caused some real problems for me or for the group. Something serious enough could have happened and cut our trip short. I had not considered the possible consequences of my decision to go. It was only later that I realized that my behavior could have affected the welfare of the entire group. I learned some valuable lessons from this experience.

Admiring a leader
Vanessa Tubbs

Shortly before my homestay in Nairobi, the Minister of Foreign Affairs, Dr. Ouko, was killed. I was living with a family on the outskirts of Nairobi at the time of Ouko's funeral. I watched members of my homestay family mourn his death. My homestay mother, Florence, and her sister, Irene, cried openly while his funeral was being televised. Later, I talked to many people in Nairobi who were also deeply saddened by his death.

I thought about how little I would be affected if someone killed an American political leader; that thought upset me. My generation of Americans, at least the students I know, don't feel that they have political leaders to respect and admire. Kenyans my age also struck me by their dedication to the growth and development of their country. So many teen-agers in my country don't seemed concerned about the welfare of America. Since my return, I have noticed that I have become more aware and concerned about what is going on in my country.

Peter, my homestay brother, told me that today we would be going to the market to buy groceries for his father's business. He worked in a little *duka* (store) in a south Nairobi suburb, and I had the pleasure of working with him during my homestay. Since the *duka* was out of fresh fruit and vegetables, we needed to take a bus to the downtown market to get them. We closed up the shop and went to the bus stop.

Being the grocer
Jonathan
Tourzan

The bus was amazingly crowded. There were about forty people on a bus with seating for only twenty. To get in or out, you simply had to push through solid masses of people. It was nothing like the empty buses that are customary in America.

We got off the bus about two blocks from the market in a very busy part of town. Lorries piled high with produce were coming in and going out of the market place. There were hundreds of men and women unloading the lorries and bringing the produce to their stands to sell. Between the stands were tiny walk-ways with room for just one person at a time.

Peter walked toward a man who was selling bananas. The bananas were green and still on the branch. Peter bought a bunch of about fifty bananas and put it over his shoulder to carry. We then went to the other side of the market, and I waited for Peter who was buying cabbage, spinach, carrots and tomatoes. We put these in a sack, and Peter gave them to me to carry.

We brought the vegetables over to a man whom Peter knew. The man had a cart onto which Peter put his vegetables. He told Peter that he would bring them down in the afternoon. The man had several customers in the same neighborhood for whom he did the same service. His job generated enough money for his family's subsistence.

We left the market and went back to the bus stop. The return bus was not as crowded, but it was still very full. Later that afternoon the vegetables came, and we displayed the fresh produce in front of the store for the customers to see.

Living with Peter was enlightening. I discovered firsthand the economic and social realities of Nairobi. In Nairobi, money is so precious. People will work hard to make pennies. This money, in turn, will buy food. I became aware of how much we take our financial resources for granted in America. I now understand that most people do not have as much as I do. This experience brought me a greater understanding of life in a developing country and helped me to see things from a global perspective.

Singing with my sister

Megan Mathias

"Jambo, Jambo bwana, habari gani, nzuri sana, ..." (Hello, Hello friend, How are you?, Very fine, ...) my homestay sister sang as she busily braided my hair. She commented on how great my hair was because it wasn't like other white girls. It was dry and thick, so the braid stayed without a rubber band. As she sang, I began to learn the words, and we sang together:

Jambo	(Hello)
Jambo bwana	(Hello mister)
Habari gani	(How are you doing)
Nzuri sana	(Very good)
Wageni	(Strangers)
Mwakari bishwa	(Welcome to our country)
Kwetu Kenya	(In our home in Kenya)
Hakuna matata	(There are no problems)
Kenya nchi nzuri	(Kenya is a beautiful country)
Hakuna matata	(There are no problems)
Kenya nchi nzuri	(Kenya is a beautiful country)
Hakuna matata	(There are no problems)

Photo: courtesy of Laura Zarcone

CHAPTER 3: LIVING WITH THE KIKUYU

Our rural homestay was in the rural district of Muranga located in fertile highlands north of Nairobi. This region was the home of the Kikuyu tribe, the largest in Kenya. Jomo Kenyatta, Kenya's first president, was a Kikuyu.

Arriving in the country Jonathan Tourzan

The Muranga District is populated by families who make a living by working a *shamba*, a *Kiswahili* word describing a small plot of land with just a few acres. The families grow staple crops, such as *maize*, beans, potatoes, bananas, and cash crops, such as coffee or tea. Muranga's rich soil and frequent rainfall make it a beautifully green and lush paradise, and one of the most fertile farming areas in Kenya.

We traveled for over an hour to reach a small town which was the end of the line for our bus. The bus dropped us off at Kandara Market where we went into a small *hotel* (restaurant) and had lunch while we waited for Maina to find a *matatu* to take us the last few miles to our destination.

The open market offered a variety of fruits and vegetables, including multicolored bananas that were particularly delicious. We were the center of attention at the market where strangers were not a common sight. I felt like everything I did would leave an impression on these people, most of who had never interacted with Americans. This made me extremely self-conscious so I decided to be playful by creating the stereotype that *Americans love fruit.* Then I bought every kind of strange fruit imaginable. I thought that our differences would make us the center of attention throughout our stay in Muranga.

**Exploring
Kandara
Andrew Lipson**

Our van pulled up the main road of the small town causing people to turn their heads and stare. White skinned people were an extreme rarity in this region, and twelve hyperactive teen-age students were enough to make people question their eyesight.

We piled out of the van, and Maina told us the basic plan. We would eat here in the *hotel,* a two-room concrete building with windows but no glass or screens. Then we would have an hour to walk about the marketplace. We ordered our meal with Maina's help, and a few even suceeded in ordering vegetarian meals. Jon Rinard was not so lucky. He got a piece of meat that he chewed on for half an hour, wondering if he could take it out of his mouth without being rude. We were always under the greatest scrutiny with what seemed like thousands of men, women, and children staring at us.

In twos and threes we left the little *hotel* to see the market. I left alone — I see myself as a loner and a rebel — and began to walk down the street toward the market. Eyes followed me, seeming to ask billions of questions: "What are these people doing here?" "What do they want?" "What is he going to do?" I knew how rare white people were in this area, and I knew that their memories of white people probably consisted of missionaries and colonists. I could hardly blame them if they were a little suspicious of me. I tried to greet them in *Kiswahili,* "*Jambo!*" and "*Habari gani!*" Maybe they only spoke Kikuyu, or maybe they did not know why I trying to talk to them. The only responses I could get were a few even stranger looks.

I turned around and walked back to the *hotel* to see if I could find some company. No one was there. It would be another forty-five minutes before we were to meet there. I started back to the market with everyone watching me.

Up ahead of me, there was a thin woman with wild hair who was yelling something at three of our students. They didn't notice her and kept on walking, so she picked up a rock and tossed it toward them. The rock landed behind them, and they walked on oblivious to it. The woman turned and started talking to me in her native language. Her face was twitching, and it occurred to me that she might not be completely sane.

I told her as well as I could that I did not understand her. Then I began to walk onward. She then shouted and made a wild gesture that I will never forget. She spun her arms in the air and kicked one leg to the side and twisted it to show me the bottom of her foot. She looked like some insane sorcerer or witch. All the town's people watching us burst out laughing.

I quickly said that I did not understand and started walking. I did not know what her gesture had meant, but I did not think it was very friendly. I went into the market and met Jon who was also alone. We walked around the market, but all I saw were people selling beans and what looked like sandals from K-Mart. I saw Dana and Megan talking to an older man. I envied them for finding a friendly person with whom they could converse.

A little while later I had a chance to talk to a man when he came up to Jon and me and started talking to us in Kikuyu. Jon and I tried to figure out what he was saying from his actions and from using the little *Kiswahili* we knew; it was just not working. He kept pointing with his cane to Jon's cola bottle, then to his hat, then to his pants that had holes in them, and then to his shoes that did not match. A crowd gathered around us, and, after what seemed hours, a young teen-ager stepped forward and said in English: "He says he wants your hat."

Jon and I looked at each other. He asked me what I should do, and I suggested that he just give this guy his hat. We walked out of the crowd hurriedly and started toward the hotel. We met Susan who told us that Paula was feeling sick and that the hotel manager had found her a quiet place to sit behind the hotel. I quickly went to join her. This was, by far, my scariest hour of the trip.

**Riding in
the matatu
Katy Arnovick**

"Three more people to go into the *matatu*. Just scoot down and squeeze in a little more!" coaxed the driver, as he stood near the back of a small, enclosed Toyota truck.

The twelve of us piled into the six-person *matatu* as the hot sun beamed down on the roof. We sat on each other's laps and squished our bodies. We were too excited to complain. We had walked a long way, and it was such a relief to reach the bus. We slowly began to move, and then, within minutes, we were speeding down a bumpy dirt road toward the homes where we would spend the next two days.

As we continued down the road, I could not see where we were going. Finally, I managed to get a glance out of a side window at the dirt road. I noticed that there was a rushing river ahead. We were going to cross over it on a narrow bridge made out of what appeared to be weak wooden planks. I instantly pictured us falling through. As we began to go over it, I held my breath in fear. I saw others around me doing the same. "AHHHH!" I finally sighed in relief; "We made it."

I knew our drop off spot was coming up because we had been traveling for what seemed like half an hour, and Maina had told us that the drive would take forty minutes. Though I was beginning to get used to our cramped conditions, I was looking forward to getting off the *matatu*. Suddenly, the bus began to shake and bump more than ever. Again I gave a quick look out of my window and saw that we were driving over large rocks used to fill the pot holes.

Everything was so strange: First cramming into a small truck/bus, and now going over rocks put in the road to fill pot holes. But I was learning to accept things and was more prepared for anything out of the ordinary. Finally, we stopped and got out of the bus. I looked around and saw beautiful trees growing out of rich red soil. I saw a house with bright green grass in the front yard, with goats and a baby cow tied up to a cage. The ride in the *matatu* was an experience I will always remember from Kenya.

I learned from my experiences in Kenya how much I take everything for granted in America: how dependent I am on all the conveniences I have, such as private bathrooms and private cars. I will also remember the people here: my family and friends. I appreciate what I have so much more now and wish others could experience what I did.

Photo: Audrey Bethke

Arriving in paradise
Julie Paiva

Muranga was the experience of a lifetime. Every moment there was something new and different going on. It started at the town of Kandara. I got out of the Toyota van and was instantly surrounded by curious faces. People watched every move I made.

I felt claustrophobic in the back of the *matatu*, and I was relieved when we finally arrived at *Baba* Maina's *shamba* — *Baba* Maina is David Maina's father. I wanted to get out of the *matatu* as fast as I could, not thinking about where I was, only about how I did not want to be inside for another minute. But, the second I stepped onto solid ground, I forgot the awful ride.

I found myself surrounded by the most beautiful country I had ever seen — the bright red dirt, the dark green trees, and the biggest, bluest sky in the world. I felt as if I were in paradise and, more than once, seriously questioned whether I was dreaming. In the fear of waking up, I quickly started running around, trying to see all that I could. I did not want to miss anything.

I walked down to a river behind *Baba* Maina's house and ran into some children along the path. I greeted them and tried to shake their hands, but they just laughed and ran away. I continued walking to the river while the children continued running up to me, touching my hands and running away. I felt so happy and so curious. Just like the children touching my hands, I wanted to touch every part of Kenya, the land and the people.

Getting acquainted
Jonathan Tourzan

The *matatu* had taken us on a bumpy ride through lush green hills to *Baba* Maina's house. In Kenya, adults are addressed as the parent of their eldest child; therefore, the name *Baba* Maina means "father of Maina." David Maina's father had played a large role in organizing our homestays in Muranga and turned out to be an invaluable friend. *Baba* Maina welcomed us to his home. He explained that our homestay families would not arrive for a while and that we were free to explore his land while we waited for our families.

The scenery in Muranga was spectacular. Green terraced hills stretched out across the land as far as I could see. Almost all the land was used to grow crops of one kind or another. *Baba* Maina's house was beautiful; he had one of the few houses with a concrete foundation in the area. There were several goats in his front yard, and on the side of the yard were two cows eating banana tree branches in a wooden cage. Below *Baba* Maina's house was a beautiful stream that cut through the valley. We walked down the *shamba* to the stream where we met a group of curious children. They would say, "How are you?" and then bashfully run away. Some of them would hide in bushes when they saw us coming and then jump out giggling after we had passed by. I think they thought that we might eat them for lunch. They were so innocent, so pure.

Back at the house, a small group of children had gathered. They had discovered that we were not there to eat them, and a few of them gathered up the courage to talk to us. They thought everything we said or did was hilarious. We played with them while we waited for our families to arrive. To my surprise, they knew how to play checkers and proved to be formidable opponents. I explained the game to them, and I

Photo: Joyce Zarcone

invited them to try it. Before I knew what had happened, my little opponent had jumped two of my pieces and made it to my side of the board. "King me!" he exclaimed in English.

Eventually, we all left *Baba* Maina's house with our homestay families. Each student stayed with a separate family and had his/her own unique experiences. The rains were just beginning, so it was planting season. Because of this, there was much work to be done on the *shamba*. Our group did such things as hoe fields, plant corn, and plant potatoes. I helped prepare one of my family's *shambas* for planting. My homestay sister and I got up early and tilled the land with hoes. Local men and women would stop and watch, some even came down and shook my hand. My sister explained that they had never seen white people do physical labor and that they were impressed. "*Wewe Kikuyu!*" (You are a Kikuyu!) they exclaimed.

Maina led our group down to the small river that ran in the draw below his *shamba*. It had a beautiful milky water, similar in color to the Mississippi. We wandered freely through the red and green patch-work hills of *maize* (corn), sweet potatoes, kale, beans, and banana trees.

Nurturing the land Laura Zarcone

It upset me when I heard that a large coffee plantation had poisoned the river. I thought that Kenyan agriculture would be free of pesticides. Looking back, it was idealistic for me to believe that their farms would be organic. I realize that, as nations struggle to develop they often adopt Western practices that have short-term benefits, yet serious long-range consequences.

**Extending
our hands
Bruce Epis**

One thing that touched me in Muranga was the innocence of the children. They were filled with so much curiosity about us. My first experience with them was when I was walking with my friend Paula and our host mothers. We were walking by a medical dispensary when some school children came running down the dirt path toward us.

They saw us and stopped suddenly; then they looked at us in awe. Paula and I each stuck out our hands, and they jumped back in fright. Many of the children had never seen white people. We blew up a balloon and gave it to them. They started to play with it and laugh. Some came up to us, shook our hands, and asked, "How are you?" We then went on to our homes. The children followed us the whole way, holding our hands and looking at us. The smiles on their faces made me feel like I belonged here.

**Staying with
the chief
Jon Rinard**

The day I set off for my first homestay was one that I will never forget. I remember the level of anxiety I felt as we climbed into the van. These questions flashed through my mind: "What will my homestay parents be like?" or "What if we can't communicate?" About an hour after we got to the village of our homestay, I saw parents leaving with some other students. The longer I stayed and waited the less anxious I became because I could sense how much these families cared. *Baba* Maina told me that I was staying with the chief of the village; I felt honored to be his only guest.

When the chief arrived, I expected him to have a traditional dress with some kind of headdress. To my surprise, when I met him, he was wearing a camouflage jacket, slacks, and a black beret. He carried a foot-long ebony rod with a small blade inside as a symbol of authority.

We started walking toward his house, but we got diverted when we got to the town. The chief was passing a record book around so that people could make payments in support of community projects. This practice is called *harambee* (pulling together) and is the principal means of community fund raising in Kenya. He talked to almost everyone in the immediate area while I stood around trying to understand their conversations.

A group of seven or eight boys gathered about ten feet from me and started whispering amongst themselves. This was something that I still had not gotten used to, and I got self-conscious. One boy asked me: "How are you?" I told him, "*Nzuri*". Another boy asked me where I was from. When I told him that I was from America, they all repeated the word slowly.

When the chief had finished collecting money, I asked him where his house was. He simply pointed and said: "Oh, it's just over there." As it turned out, it took us a little over an hour to get there. During the walk to his house, we talked about my family and America. The famous question that he asked, that I will never forget, was "What is your major cash crop?" It took me a little while to convince him that my family did not farm to survive and that my mom had a job.

When we reached the house, I was surprised by how little time we spent before leaving again. After I had dropped off my bag, the chief and his two sons took me to see the coffee factory. We arrived after a half hour walk. The chief showed me all the parts of the factory. I saw where the beans arrive, where they are washed, and where they are stored before they are loaded into the trucks.

At this point, the sun was setting, and it was almost dark. The chief wanted to visit a friend's house; "Just over there," so, once again, away we went, with me following the chief. A good half-hour later, we arrived at a house that looked much like the chief's. We went inside and sat around a table. The chief and his woman friend talked for a long time in their tribal language, Kikuyu. Then his friend started asking me questions in her language; the chief translated for me. She asked me all about America and asked me if I had brought anything from America. I got out my passport and some money from the U.S.; they were all interested and passed the articles around and talked about each one. During this stay, I found out how hospitable Kenyans are. Every time I finished a cup of tea, they would immediately refill it. I eventually drank six or seven cups before leaving.

Soon, it was time to leave, so we said "*Kwa heri*" (good-bye) and headed back to the chief's house. It was pitch dark, but my brothers could see perfectly well. They practically guided me all the way home.

When we got back, we went inside and sat around the table. My homestay mother served our dinner, and we drank some more tea. After attempting to finish a huge dish of *ugali* (corn mush) and beef, I gave up. The chief wanted to know some more about the U.S., so I gave him a book with many pictures of California. He browsed through it, promising to read it later. It was getting late by then, so my two brothers and I went out to the other building, about twenty feet away, to go to sleep. Since there were only two beds, they had doubled up so that I could have a bed to myself.

The next morning, I woke up and put on a t-shirt and some pants. It felt about seventy degrees, and I was enjoying the coolest weather since our arrival. My brother came up to me, bundled in a sweater and shivering and asked me if the cold bothered me. He was really surprised when I told him that back in California, it was much colder than this.

We started back to the central homestay house a little while later. Although I spent half a day and one night with them, I will never forget that night we gathered around the table by the kerosene lantern, drinking tea and talking about a place far away that I called home.

I believe that my Muranga family and I made a strong connection. I felt especially close to my three Kenyan brothers — Titus (fifteen), Daniel (sixteen), and George (seventeen) — because we were close to the same age.

Breaking through color
Jesse Baumgartner

One night we stayed up late in my small, dusty room. It was one of the three rooms my family had for thirteen people; I could not believe that they all fit in their home. My house is twice as big and only two people live in it. My brothers and I talked about many things — the girls we like at school, our different governments, marriage customs, and family structures. I felt comfortable with my brothers, and I could tell from their openness that they felt the same way.

A young Kikuyu boy about ten years old came to the hut that night to buy milk from my family. I was the first white person whom he had ever seen. Surprised and curious, he asked questions about my journey to their village, while my brothers translated. He touched my long hair and pinched my skin to see if I was real. Then he offered to kill a rabbit to honor my presence in Kenya. I explained to him that the offer touched me, but that my purpose was to live as they did. I also told him that I did not want him to do anything special for me just because of the color of my skin. One of my brothers said softly: "Although we are different colors, our blood is the same, and we are brothers."

The walls consist of hardened red mud; the floor is simply red earth. As I enter the room, I feel a slight breeze, like an underground coolness. The surrounding earth gives me a refreshing feeling. I can feel my primitive instincts, which developed long before shoes became a barrier between man and the earth. I hear a gentle voice say something that I cannot understand. It's my host mother. My brother Martin calls back "ehhhhhh," (this is equivalent to "uh-huh" in our culture) in his deep voice.

Laughing with my brothers
Dana Jensen

There are two beds placed side by side. I'm sitting on the edge of one bed next to my brother Martin. On the other bed, Simon and Charles are sitting with their friend Joseph. There is a boy next to me who does not speak a word. He just watches as we talk about our two countries.

Martin pulls out a scrabble board from beneath the bed. It surprises me to see something so familiar, especially since we were just talking about everything being so different. I am now struck by how we are also alike. We divide the wooden blocks and start to play. My brothers show their intelligence through their vocabulary and quickness. Joseph is having a little trouble, so we help him out; he gracefully accepts.

The game eventually fades away as we get into an in-depth conversation about the roles of men and women. I feel safe about what I am saying; I know that I can be completely honest as I reveal some secret parts of my life. I become excited as we learn from each other about our different lifestyles.

I tell them that I do not like the way men treat women in Kenya. "How come men don't listen to women and don't think that they can do many things?" I ask. Then they explain to me the respect given to women for what they do. They also become excited and smile, because they see that I am openly expressing my opinions. I feel that they respect me now in a different way.

When I tell them that in America I am free to do or say what I want, they are both shocked and impressed. Charles tells me, "You are very smart," and starts to giggle. His two brothers join in and soon we are all smiling and laughing.

Teaching one another
Leah Mowery

It is night time in a dark room with one kerosene lantern. I sit at a small wooden table with five children and my homestay sister. The lamp lights the room, but darkness crowds in the corners; I can barely make out objects ten feet away from me. I look at the beautiful, innocent faces of the children who timidly ask me for help with their math. They give me an old workbook to write in, and I go through the problems, explaining everything. I wonder how much of this they already know or if they even understand what I am doing. When I finish, they thank me and go on with their work; I wonder again if I helped.

Books clutter the small table, overlapping each other, and each child tries to get enough room to write. I watch them as they write; they write slowly with meticulous care. It's as if they know how necessary their education is and take great care with it, down to every written letter. The children are working on separate assignments, yet they take the time to help each other. Homework is a family activity; a math problem gets started but then is put down because a brother is not doing his English assignment correctly. There is a continuous murmur going on between them about the work that they are doing. I do not understand exactly what they are saying, but I can tell that they are sharing different opinions while they try to find the correct solution. The mother is there too, collaborating on the answers.

One girl, Ema, detaches herself from her brothers and sisters and does work in a music book alone. She gets bumped at times, or arms reach past her, but she stays at her homework, intensely concentrating on the words.

A part of me wishes that homework could be like this at my home. I can imagine myself alone in my room, working on my assignments, and I compare it to this scene of children crowding around a single light. Though my room is filled with luxuries, it lacks this feeling of support and togetherness.

Hanging out with Francis
Ryan Marton

It was early morning. My homestay brother Francis awakened me saying: "It's time to get up! We've got to go plant some potatoes today in the field behind the house." I got up and went with him. Our first job was to milk the cow. Francis watched me and talked to me as I took my turn. I found it easy to talk to Francis. We had much in common since we were the same age. After we finished milking, we headed for the field.

As I stepped onto the earth, the soft, red dirt gave way and my bare feet sank to my ankles. Each move that I made sent black crickets running everywhere. I could not help stepping on them, but I got used to them as we worked.

Photo: Francis Maina

Francis and I planted potatoes and talked all morning. He told me that if he came to America he would get a red, yellow, and green lion tattooed on his arm. Those are the colors that symbolize the Rastas, he explained.

We finished work and went to a nearby chicken feed store to hang out with his friends. We sat around and talked about girls. Francis said he had taken a college entrance exam, but he was afraid that he had not passed. There are only four universities in the country and just a handful of students get to go. Francis was not sure what he would do next. He said that he might become a linguistics instructor like his uncle but that he would need to learn German and French to do this.

That evening after we ate, we went to town to buy tea leaves, and it started to rain heavily. It had rained every night of my homestay and I always got stuck in the rain somewhere. This time we huddled outside the four shops that made the town waiting for it to quit. After it rained for fifteen minutes, the water had flooded the ground. When we finally walked home, it was like walking in a river. We had to jump from rock to rock to avoid the potholes that covered the road. Having spent two days here, I was used to walking home like this. Muranga was beginning to feel like home to me. I felt happy in my house even though it was made of mud; I felt so safe here.

Walking through the black hallway, I did not know what to expect. Domitillah, my homestay cousin, said that we were going to the kitchen, and I knew it would be nothing like my kitchen in America. We got to the doorway and walked into a small room, illuminated by a lantern. Then we boiled water over a small fire in the middle of the room. Sitting on a wooden bench, I noticed the dirt floors and mud walls. The smoke from the fire filled the room with no way to escape.

Domitillah brought me some bananas and sat down beside me on the bench. She introduced me to the six children in the room. Although I could not see their faces, I saw their eyes watching me through the darkness. The hard rain was pounding against the tin roof, making it difficult to hear each other's voices. I was so far away from my family and friends in America, yet I felt at home. Still, I could not cover up my shock of being surrounded by this culture which was so new to me. At that moment, I became filled with the realization that I was in Kenya. I knew I was on the other side of the world. I had so much joy inside me; I felt like crying.

The girl watching the fire handed me some *maize* that she had cooked over the open fire. Everyone smiled and watched me as I tried to figure out how to eat it. Domitillah finally showed me; it tasted good. The girl by the fire watched me very closely. When I noticed her, she smiled and hid her face; I wanted to speak to her but could not. Even if I could have, I would not have known what to say. These people lead lives so different from mine, but, when we smiled at each other, we shared the same warmth.

The smoke burned my eyes; the children began to cry; the rain started to fall even harder. I felt scared, but not for my life; I knew that I was not in danger. I felt confused. I did not know how to interpret everything I was seeing. I explained that I was very tired and asked Domitillah to walk me to my room. Lying in bed that night, I realized that something inside me had changed and that I would never be the same.

**Being with
Monica
Susan
Abramson**

For ten years, I had wanted to go to Africa, having heard about it in stories and books. When Gary said that I could go along as a chaperon, I was very happy and excited. There were many discomforts and challenging moments that called for the best and the worst of me, but it was the most exciting and satisfying nineteen days of my life.

When I was in the rural district of Muranga, I stayed with a Kikuyu woman about my age named Monica. Monica was a leader among the women in the village, organizing the dispensary, and leading the local women in various community projects.

When Monica came to walk me home, her liveliness impressed me immediately. She had sparkle and fire in her eyes; she moved her slender body with great agility. She walked briskly, stopping often to greet other villagers, and laughing almost non-stop. Her laughter was so infectious that I soon found myself joining in. She spoke no English and only a few words of *Kiswahili*, so our eye contact and body language had to suffice for communication.

On the way to her farm, she showed me many sights including some of her friends' homesteads, a little creek, and her brother's small market. Here, she told me that I could have anything I desired. I took a candle and thanked her brother. Each time she introduced me to a new person, she would tell me how to make the greeting, "*We mwe ga*." And, each time I said it, she and her friends would explode with laughter; I never did pronounce it right.

At the farm, I had trouble keeping up with this woman who was always running up and down the dirt tiers of her land. She would stop and look back at me with her beautiful smile. She was truly athletic and energetic. She stopped here and there to plant a seed that magically came out of her pockets, or to pull a potato out of the ground, or to pick an ear of corn. This collection later proved to be our dinner. She took me to her homestead which consisted of four small huts, centered around a water tank and a patch of mud.

We went into the kitchen to prepare the evening meal. The kitchen was a small hut with a dirt floor. Monica had three *burners* built against the back wall. This was different from the traditional set of three rocks used to support cooking pots in

Photo: Susan Abramson

most rural kitchens. Monica's stove had three cement holes with cast iron covers to keep the pots over the fire. On the way to the kitchen, Monica had picked up some firewood. She had two fires going by the time I sat next to her on a small stool. Surveying the dark kitchen, I saw chickens nesting on the ground, children staring at me with wide eyes, stools, and a wooden cabinet with wire mesh doors for food storage.

I prepared the dinner meal with Monica and her daughters, using a small dull knife to peel about two hundred tiny potatoes. It took me forever, and I kept thinking that I would like to send them a potato peeler when I returned to the U.S.. I know that they thought I was very slow. I wanted to tell them that I was not accustom to using such a dull knife, but, alas, I had no way to talk to them. We laughed until my sides hurt about the antics of the grandchildren and the joy of simply being together. I felt very welcome in Monica's kitchen.

Later her two sons came and sat with us in her bedroom hut, and we looked at the few pictures that they had. The sons spoke some English, so we could exchange some ideas and get answers to some of the questions that we both had. She wanted to know how many cows I had, how I cooked in my kitchen, and what my husband and family were like. She told me that her husband was away in Nairobi working. She wanted to know what sorts of things I grew in my garden and what I grew for a cash crop. She was impressed when I told her that I worked in an office for money.

I felt sad when it was time for me to leave. There was a camaraderie that I felt with her and her daughters that I will never forget. I told her how impressed I was with her farm and her achievements. I told her that I would never forget this time with her and that I thought she was a remarkable woman. I can still see her bright laughing eyes and hear her warm laughter.

Remembering moments
Katy Arnovick

Imagine yourself in a dark, cold room with a hard dirt floor. Nearby is a pot, cooking some food that you can not quite make out. Now imagine six children staring up at you with big innocent eyes. Rain is pouring down; it sounds like tons of ripe cherries falling from a tree.

This is a description of a typical kitchen in a little village about fifty miles north of Nairobi. It was in such a village that I enjoyed one of my best experiences in Kenya.

I have such strong memories of sitting in the dark hut, walls made of mud, floors made of earth. I remember that there was no electricity and only a tiny dim lantern to see by. This experience helped me to see the dramatic difference between our two cultures. It also helped me to appreciate how many conveniences we have in America.

Though our worlds were different, I found that inside we were very much alike. I shared many common goals and interests with my host family in Muranga. I realized that it was extremely easy to connect and relate with these people. Throughout my stay, they showed a genuine caring toward me. When I left, I knew that I had become very attached and close to my family. I still think about them daily, and I often wonder if I will ever see them again.

Cooking dinner with my homestay mother, Anastasia, was amazing. Preparing dinner took a long time because we only had a few pots that my mother had to wash and then reuse. She had to carry the water to wash them from a community faucet outside. We were going to have a stew of potatoes, pumpkin, peas and *ugali*, so my mother gave me a pot of potatoes to peel.

To peel the potatoes, I sat on a wooden bench on top of a dirt floor with mud walls behind me and a fire stove in front of me. I knew that I was in a culture that had lived the same way for generations. My mother and I would look up from time to time and just laugh. We were both amazed that I was really there.

**Cooking with
my mother
Julie Paiva**

I joined my homestay mother and her eight children in a small wooden building to escape the rain. In the center was a pot of boiling water heated by a stone fire. My throat burned from the smoke filling the room, and my eyes strained to see in the darkness. As I sat on a handmade wooden bench on the dirt floor, all I could hear was the pounding of rain on the metal roof. Feelings of warmth and innocence washed over me as my eyes gazed over the faces of my family. All nine pairs of eyes fixed on me with curiosity.

**Running fingers
Jenelle Flaherty**

I turned to look out at the rain through the window. As I felt the cool air on my face, I also felt little fingers running through my hair. I quickly turned back to see three children full of innocent laughter hide their faces and hurry toward their seats. Although these unfamiliar faces seemed different from mine, we shared a very special experience together.

Looking up at the sky
Jesse Baumgartner

My mind has opened like an endless envelope here.
Inside the knowledge gained abounds.
My eyes gazing deep.
The sky shimmering with
    Raven Gray Clouds.
My Aura gleaming into the Earth,
    and the Entire Universe.
My ears arise to the Harmony
    of the Village.
The refreshing rain falling upon my lips.
And the Red Sun fell into the Red Earth
And the sweet rain caressed
    my throat.
And I looked up into the sky.

Being a Black American
Vanessa Tubbs

Being one of two Black-Americans on this trip, I had a somewhat different experience than the rest of the students with whom I journeyed.

Many of the people who lived in Kenya could not believe that I was an American. They had learned in school about the slave trade, but they thought that most slaves had died on the trading ships going to America. So when I told the families with whom I stayed about myself and from where I came, I had to tell them some history of America so that they could understand my heritage.

I remember when I was staying in Muranga my home stay brother, Maina (not our host), took me for a walk. We talked about many things regarding race. I told him about the plight of the American Indians. He asked me if there were many of them living in my country today. I told him that many tribes had disappeared but that there were still some Indians trying to maintain a tribal identity. This fact upset Maina, and he told me that many of his people had changed to Western ways and were also losing their culture.

I also told him about Martin Luther King. I was very surprised to discover that he had not heard of him. I told him about the sit-ins, about the bus boycotts, and the other civil rights protests. I told him about the Civil War and how black people are still striving for equality.

I also told him about the problems facing our Black-American youth today, such as drug abuse, gang violence, and teen pregnancy. He seemed very concerned. We walked and talked for nine hours comparing our two countries. We finally came to the conclusion that we both came from beautiful countries and that we still had many obstacles to overcome.

Baba Maina lives in Nairobi where he owns and runs a grocery store. He spent his youth on his father's farm in the Muranga District, and he still owns a potion of the six-acre family farm. It was there that he hosted some members of our group during our rural homestays.

Baba Maina is a highly respected elder in Muranga. Although he grew up under the British colonial rule, he is a man with strong ties to his native Kikuyu tradition. Still, he chooses western ways and generally wears a suit and tie, even when at his country home.

At night, we would sit around the fire and talk about Kikuyu history and tradition. Baba Maina is a very proud man who is changing with the times and moving forward. Yet, he remembers and respects the old ways.

Talking to Baba Maina
Ryan Martin

I find it difficult to explain why I respect someone so deeply when I only knew him for a short while. *Baba* Maina was our host in Muranga. I remember whispering to my friend when I first saw him: "I like that man, his smile is honest and loving." He truly touched my heart when we gave him one of the Peace

Presenting the Wreath
Jesse Baumgartner

Photo: Katy Arnovick

Wreaths that we had brought with us to Kenya. His face flushed with appreciation as he explained how much the wreath meant to his village. Although we had just met, *Baba* Maina brought us into his home and told us: "Whatever I have is yours; let my home be your home." He is such a beautiful person.

Bringing peace messages
Jenelle Flaherty

I wish that all those people who donated money to me could have been there to see *Baba* Maina hold up his community's Peace Wreath with such great pride. I wish that everyone could have seen the two Muranga mothers as they eagerly read all the messages that we brought with us. They smiled happily, and I could tell that the two of them could feel the love that the Wreaths carried. It brings me joy to realize that these colorful Peace Wreaths will remain in Kenya with all our friends, even though we will have to return home.

My great grandmother came out of her hut to greet me as I was leaving Muranga. She clasped my hand and grinned her toothless smile. She spoke to me in her tribal language, Kikuyu, with her shining black eyes staring into my blue ones.

Her granddaughter translated for me: "You are welcome in my home. You be free and happy here. You are so kind. Come again. Good-bye. You are always welcome in my family." I was struck by her friendliness. I had never met her before, yet she was so kind and accepting. I felt like I was part of her family.

Saying good-bye
Fiona Hollins

While we were waiting for the van that would take us back to Nairobi, Julie and I met a group of children. None of them spoke English, and we did not speak much of their language, Kikuyu. At first we did not approach them because we were excited to be returning to the YMCA where we would rejoin the rest of our group. Yet, when we looked around at the red soil and adobe buildings in the small marketplace, we realized that we would miss Muranga.

Reaching the
children
Katy Arnovick

I remembered that one of our goals for this trip had been to relate with the children and to gain a better understanding of the Kenyan culture. I knew that I did not want to lose this opportunity, so I approached the children. At first we just stared at each other. This brought smiles to all their faces and even enticed some more children to join our group.

As usual, there were about eight children surrounding us, watching everything we did. I usually just ignored them because of the language barrier, but, this time, I felt the need to connect with them somehow.

Leaving the
children
Julie Paiva

For lack of a better idea, Katy and I began making silly faces at them. At first they were shocked, but, slowly, one by one, the children started making the same faces at us. Then Ian and Heather joined us, and we began singing traditional American songs. We started with *Little Bunny Fufu*. The children could not understand the words, but they watched us, intrigued by the singing. We continued to sing traditional children's songs as more children gathered around.

Katy gave her bracelet to a little girl with a baby on her back; then I gave one of my shirts to another little girl. The shirt had a picture of palm trees on it and *Santa Barbara* written across it. It was a normal sized shirt on me, but it looked like a dress on her. She stood there with her mouth wide open, looking up at me in amazement. Her friends all giggled as she turned around to show them. She looked so cute. I wanted to take her home with me, but I could not. Katy took a picture of her, and we shook hands to say good-bye. The *matatus* had come, and, although I was not ready to leave, I grudgingly picked up my pack and got into the van.

Leaving a legacy
Jonathan
Tourzan

While we were staying in the Muranga District, the District Chief showed us their partially built medical dispensary. These local people had been working for several years to raise enough money to complete the construction of the dispensary to provide medical care for people in their local farming community.

The chief explained that the nearest facilities were twenty kilometers away. If anyone in the village were sick, it would be very difficult for him/her to get treatment as there was only one car in the vicinity, and this car was often in use. The dispensary was almost completed, but the building of a new school and church had competed for funds. The chief told us that when they raised the remaining $1750 the government would provide medical supplies and a trained staff for the dispensary. This worthy project appealed greatly to us.

We had decided before we came to Kenya that we were going to give a scholarship to a young student from Muranga. During our stay, we got to meet the girl who would receive the support, Alice Ndura. Alice was an excellent student. Her parents were burdened by having to support eight children with the income from a small farm. We offered to help remove some of this burden by financing her secondary education.

On the third day our homestays were finished. We met that morning at *Baba* Maina's house where we said good-bye to our homestay families. Our group gave one of our colorful Peace Wreaths decorated with messages of goodwill to *Baba*

Maina. The beautiful gift touched *Baba* Maina. After eating some sweet potatoes, we took our baggage up the road to the village center where we met the van that took us back to Nairobi.

Alice accompanied us when we returned to Nairobi. There, we got to know her in a more personal way. I talked extensively to Alice at the YMCA and found her to be a bright and forthright young girl. I was glad that we were helping her with her education.

I was riding back to the YMCA from Muranga, anxious to rejoin the rest of our group after their rural and urban homestays. I noticed that having to leave my homestay family made me sad. This feeling surprised me, especially as I recalled how scared I was when I first met my homestay family. How close I had grown to them in such a short time.

Homing in on thoughts
Dana Jensen

Laura suddenly interrupted my thoughts by shouting: "Let's not tell the urban group about Muranga or what we did." As we discussed this over the drone of wind and engine sounds, we decided that we did not want to take away from their valuable experience by revealing the details of ours. I did not exactly like the idea because I was so excited to tell everyone how incredible my stay had been; I wanted to share my special stories.

An idea occurred to me that lessened my disappointment. I suggested that we reply to any question our other group asked about Muranga by uttering in a low throaty voice, "Ehhh . . . ." This sound was something our returning group could relate to instantly. It was a very common reply among the locals of Muranga, somewhat like "Yeah" in the U.S., except stronger, more expressive and sustained. My suggestion created a roar of agreement and laughter as we all started looking at each other, humming "Ehhh." I felt smug for coming up with this idea and turned and gazed out my window.

As I reflected on my homestay family, I felt an unexpected wave of homesickness. I struggled to compensate by opening the window, letting the wind whip across my face and through my hair. I began to think ahead in time. I squinted into the

---

wind and imagined the blur of the country side to be a threshold into my next adventure. As we drove on, the beautiful country landscape transformed into city landscape. I realized that I must push ahead to new experiences. It was important for me to touch my feelings and prepare myself for new experiences.

**Getting back
on track
Heather Hoppas**

Our group was tense when we returned from our second homestay. At school in the U.S., we had weekly group meetings — we call them interpersonals — to discuss our feelings and resolve our issues. It is during this special time that we can bring up emotional problems — things in our personal lives or situations in the group that make us feel angry or sad. Interpersonals give us an opportunity to be heard, get moral support, or actually work on solving problems within the group.

Our itinerary in Kenya had been so full that we had not had a chance to bring up personal issues or to get support from the group since leaving home. Finally on our return from our homestays, we were able to set aside some time to have an interpersonal.

One student expressed her concern that people had been breaking commitments. Our commitments were our underlying agreements that enabled our group to function and to travel halfway around the world as a cohesive group. Now some of or agreements were not being kept. Students were arriving late for meetings, getting on one another's nerves, not being completely honest, forming factions, not following directives, and, most importantly, not taking responsibility to see that the group's commitments were being kept.

As some students began to admit that they had broken commitments, others reacted. Some were surprised; others expressed hurt and anger. There was a basic feeling of betrayal and disappointment within the group. We all talked about how we were feeling and what was going on to make our group function poorly. An intense period of honest exchanges left several members of our group crying, consoling, and hugging; it was an emotionally-charged time for everyone. The discussion continued for about two hours before we resolved our issues and headed back to our rooms. We were exhausted from a day of travel and an evening of confrontation, but comforted that we had regained our group trust and support.

This encounter provided me with some hard lessons on the value of commitment. I did not like the feeling in our group when people were being dishonest; now I know how much better it feels to tell the truth. That night our group decided to recommit and start anew. After our interpersonal, we were much more relaxed and ready to move forward. As I lay on my bed that night, I realized that these lessons would always be with me.

Photo: Gary Bacon

Sharing time with Alice
Fiona Hollins

Alice Ndura, a young Kikuyu, had come fifty miles to be with us in Nairobi at the YMCA. Our room was dark, and the warm fragrant air came in through the open window. We talked together about our families and our favorite classes in school. I felt very close to her as we whispered to each other. As we discussed our vocational plans—Alice wants to become a teacher—I was drawn to her inner strength and beauty. She spoke in a calm, gentle voice and was quiet but engaging. Alice was spending the evening with us in Nairobi, and I noticed that being with twenty-four Americans did not intimidate her.

She joined us during our interpersonal. I was concerned that she would get upset since our interpersonals get pretty emotional sometimes. Instead, she watched with great interest as members of our group shared anger, disappointment, remorse, support, and love. Our evening ended with people holding one another while crying and carrying out quiet conversations. When we asked her how she felt about the evening, she answered: "I am fine." Then she asked innocently: "Is this [the interpersonal] one of the customs in your country?"

Alice is only 14 years old, the first member of her family of nine siblings to attend high school. Her school in Thika costs several hundred dollars a year. Her parents had to take out a loan on their small farm to pay for her first year of high school; now our group is going to help pay for the rest of her high school education.

As Alice and I lay awake talking, I felt excited to be making a difference in her life. My life in America is so easy in comparison; my family lacks financial worries, and my education is free. I was also happy to get to know Alice. When we said good-bye, she told me: "I am so glad to be friends. You are a good girl." I have already written to her twice, and I am glad to know that I have a friend on the other side of the world.

Photo: Gary Bacon

CHAPTER 4: OVERCOMING ALL BARRIERS

The next day we set off for the Outward Bound Mountain School at Loitokitok, a small village at the base of Mount Kilimanjaro. Three vans met us at the YMCA to take us on our excursion. On our way, we drove through Amboseli Game Park, one of Kenya's richest refuges for wildlife and one of the best elephant habitats in Kenya. There we saw a variety of animals including giraffes, elephants, zebras, and wildebeests. We stopped for lunch at a *safari* (journey) lodge where we

Settling into Outward Bound
Jonathan Tourzan

came to the shocking realization that most tourists in Kenya stay at lodges and have little or no interaction with the native people. We felt out of place in this luxurious setting.

On the way to Loitokitok, a small storm broke out and turned the narrow, dirt road on which we were driving into a river of mud. At this point, one of our vans was considerably ahead of the other two. It proceeded without problems to the Outward Bound School near Loitokitok, but the other two vans got stuck on the road. Our two chaperones were getting worried because the sun was setting, and it would soon be night in this strange foreign environment. Fortunately, Steven Mc-Cormick, the only American working with the Outward Bound School, came to our aid. Steven pulled the van out of the mud with his Land-Rover, and, soon after, both vans arrived safely at the Outward Bound School.

Our group was going to join the National Youth Service (NYS) for three days of rugged outdoor activities at the six-thousand foot level of Mt. Kilimanjaro. NYS is a group of young Kenyans, ages sixteen to twenty-nine, enlisted in a training program similar to the Civilian Conservation Corps that existed in the U.S. in the 1930's. The Kenyans receive paramilitary and civil-construction training before performing essential jobs in the development of their country. At the end of a two year tour of duty, they are placed in government or civilian jobs. The NYS Kenyans are patriotic, disciplined, intelligent, and hard working.

The Outward Bound School (OBS) compound was shaped like a horseshoe. The mess hall and showers were at the top while residential halls lined the side. In the middle of the horseshoe was a garden and a flag pole flying the Kenyan flag.

After our arrival at the school, Steven told us to put our luggage into a large cabin and to come to the mess hall for dinner. The cabin had eleven bunk beds in rows with shelves for our packs. Each student took a bed and unloaded his/her pack before going to the mess hall.

At the mess hall, we were issued spoons. If we lost these spoons, we would have to eat with our hands or buy new ones. Steven warned us about the school. He told us that the days would be very strenuous, and some activities, such as the difficult parts of the ropes course, would be beyond our capacity. Steven stressed that we were not compelled to participate in any activity that we thought was beyond our means, but he encouraged us to test ourselves and to discover our capabilities. Before we went to bed, we were assigned to patrols consisting of Kenyans and Americans. In the morning, we would be participating in our activities with these small groups.

After the meeting, Steven walked down to our cabins and told us to get a good night's sleep. He told us that we would be getting up at 5:55 A.M.; then he left. He had no way of knowing that we were going to be awakened much sooner. The recent rains had caused *Siafu* (biting ants), or *Safari* Ants, to uproot and seek higher ground. Our dry cabin was exactly what they were looking for. Unbeknownst to us, thousands of these large ants began to head for our cabin.

Invading Safari Ants
Rebecca Sugg

We have had a long day. Seven hours of pushing *matatus* through the mud is not my idea of easy traveling. We have just arrived at the Outward Bound school on Mt. Kilimanjaro, and I am thinking to myself how great a full stomach and a soft bed are going to feel. I wearily walk into our cabin, choosing what I think will be the best bed in the house, knowing little about the uninvited guests who would soon claim it. When my head hit the pillow, I was fast asleep.

At four in the morning, I was rudely awakened by a sting on the side of my neck. Then another sting . . . and more, on my eyelid, in my ear; there were ants crawling in my hair. "Ouch, slap, ouch, slap, slap, slap, what the . . .?" I was trying to protect myself, and I wondered if I was the only one getting bitten.

My struggle and the army of ants began to get some attention. Jon Rinard, who was sleeping diagonal from me, whispered loudly, "Hey, Rebecca, what the hell are these things anyway?" Then people all around me started slapping and yelling and shuffling. The noise woke up the rest of the group, but, unfortunately, they were not very understanding.

"Shut up!" someone yelled from the other side of the room.

"Be quiet! It's no big deal; go back to sleep," pleaded another classmate from a lower bunk.

"You guys are exaggerating," was the muffled response from inside a nearby sleeping bag.

"Yeah, right!" I thought. Here we are getting devoured by these things, and all that people can think about is sleeping. Finally, we decided to find out for ourselves what was attacking us. Jon turned on his flashlight; now everyone started screaming, yelling, and running to the other side of the room. The huge streams of *Safari* Ants had made themselves at home, covering half the room; they had attached themselves to everything in their sight! Some had even gotten into our sleeping bags. Nobody got much sleep after that on our first night at Outward Bound.

Teaching the NYS to swim
Dana Jenson

The next morning after our ordeal with the ants, we had to get up at 5:55 A.M. for the run-and-dip ritual. I crawled out of bed to find my classmates doing warm-up exercises with the NYS. It was so dark outside that I could hardly see the OBS instructor leading the exercises, so I watched the people around me and tried to follow. One instructor with a strong tribal accent yelled: "Squat, face your partner, and jump! One! Two! Three!" I reluctantly started jumping. After the warm-ups, we ran half a mile up and down a bumpy dirt road. I was on the verge of collapse, hoping to be unnoticed, when I felt someone pushing on my back. It was a Kenyan, encouraging me to keep up with him.

I followed him to the swimming pool. It was light now, and I could see that my patrol was already there. The morning activity seemed to put everyone in a good mood. I smiled at the irony of hitting cold water at 6:20 A.M. with nothing familiar around me but my clothing and my classmates. The supervisors, standing on the opposite side of the pool; told us to stand on the deep end and to help the Kenyans get across the pool, some of them did not know how to swim. The tough Kenyans, who were good runners and disciplined, seemed so vulnerable as we got ready to jump.

"Step up! And jump!" yelled the supervisor. All but four people jumped into the pool. Then I noticed my classmate, Fiona, pushing a big Kenyan to the side of the pool; I realized that she needed help. He was thrashing in panic. I suddenly felt a rush of energy; I took a deep breath and went underwater. I swam beneath him and pushed him to the side of the pool. His head was hanging down, and his dark colored muscles flexed to cling to the side of the pool. When he had caught his breath, he looked up at me with wide eyes. I smiled at him and watched his expression turn into a huge grin.

Photo: Gary Bacon

Running the course
Jonathan Tourzan

After the run-and-dip, we had time to change for breakfast. Breakfast was simple and consisted of bread and chai, brewed with milk and sugar. One patrol was the duty patrol, and they were in charge of meal clean-up and preparation. A group meeting finished the morning routine. The meeting began with the duty patrol reviewing the news for the day. Then, someone read announcements about individual and group achievements. A thought for the day followed. This exercise consisted of an Outward Bound instructor reading a passage on a subject, such as courage or cooperation. Finally, we sang songs, usually of a religious nature — *Soldier in the Army of the Lord*, *Paul and Simon*, *Heaven Right Now*, and *Paradiso*. This type of devotional singing played a prominent part in the religious life of these young Kenyans.

Then regular activities started, these were three activities in which my patrol participated:

1) Circuit Course: This was a timed aerobic training exercise with several stations. In one station students would squat, hold a board over their head, and come to a standing position. This activity was repeated ten times. At a second station, students

would do twenty jumping pull-ups. At a third station, students had to swing on a rope and then push off a wall with their feet. This was repeated three times. Other stations included sit-ups, jumping-dips, and calf-lifts. Our Kenyan partners would count for us at each station and encourage us to try harder. Each runner did each station three times and received a time after completion.

2) The Wall: Each patrol faced the task of scaling a large wall about fifteen feet high. The rules were that no one could talk and that only two people could stand on a platform on top to help pull up people. These two had to reach the top of the wall before they could help anyone else up the wall. We lifted the first person who stood on a Kenyan's shoulders. This first person then pulled himself up without help from above. We repeated this process, at first with one person, and then with two people, pulling from the top. The last person had no shoulders on which to climb. He had to jump up and grab the outstretched hands of two men on top. They would then pull him up, thus completing the exercise. Afterward, we evaluated our work and discussed how we could have been more effective. Working together without talking bonded us with the Kenyans. We learned to relate to each other without words, and this deepened the connection between us.

3) Acid Lake: In this activity, one of the patrol members was to be blindfolded. The instructor, Evans, blindfolded one man and took us to the Acid Lake, a grass circle with a fifteen foot diameter. The circle had an avocado in the middle and a tree on one end. Evans explained that the avocado would cure the man's blindness, but, to get it, we could not touch any ground within the circle. Finally, he told us that only the blind man could get the avocado, and the lake would destroy any part of his body that contacted its toxic waters. He gave us two long sturdy ropes, five minutes to plan, and twenty minutes to execute our plan.

My group tied the two long ropes around the tree so that both the ropes were parallel and at the same height. We swung the ropes over the lake to find the position of the avocado relative to the ropes. We then brought the ropes back, outside the circle, and put the blind individual, Barasa, on the ropes at a perpendicular angle. We slowly swung him over with six people holding each rope on one end, and the tree supporting the rope on the opposite end. Another Kenyan directed the hand of Barasa: "up . . . to the left . . . no straight down!" Barasa grabbed the avocado, and we swung him back outside Acid Lake. We then evaluated and discussed how we could have done better.

It was one of my favorite exercises because it made us work together and pull for a disabled member of the group. The instructor compared the blind man to someone with a physical or a mental handicap that could not be overcome without the help of others. "We must help the handicapped even when it's difficult," said Evans.

Our patrols also did a rope's course, planning activities, map reading, swimming, and running. Each activity gave us plenty of opportunity to interact with the NYS students. We had breaks for tea and lunch. Before dinner, we had our evening run to build up our appetites. This was the last of our activities, and our evenings were free after dinner. During this time we could

Photos: Gary Bacon

socialize, do our washing, or clean up around the cabin.

The next day started out in similar fashion with the run-and-dip, breakfast, and morning meeting. After this, all the Americans went with two of the four Kenyan patrols to the high wall. Here, Steven and the other instructors taught us some basic rock climbing techniques. The big wall was made of two thirty foot platforms with one placed on top of the other. The platforms were almost perpendicular to the ground. Between the two platforms was a ledge parallel to the ground. Each platform had blocks which one could use for pulling oneself up or as footholds for support. The climber was belayed with a rope held by two people on the ground, usually one of our students and a NYS person. We each scaled the front of the wall and rappelled down the back.

Afterward, we met with Steven and went over what the next few days would be like. He told us that we were going to hike about fifteen kilometers to a nearby Maasai village where we would visit a primary school and meet with the villagers. He warned us that if it rained the hike would become difficult, as we would be walking knee-deep in mud.

Learning from Steven

Laura Zarcone

The first evening at Outward Bound when Steven McCormick gave us his gung-ho speech about "breaking an ankle," I kept a skeptical watch on him. The olive drab uniforms of the NYS people and the boot camp atmosphere of the Mountain School increased my skepticism.

"Great!" I thought; "I'm part of a fascist plot to teach unity and cooperation through physical cruelty. It is going to be administered by the Kenyan staff, and our National Youth Service counterparts will humiliate us in every event." That night nestled in my cot, I wondered who had planned our little excursion to Outward Bound. "It was Jonathan; that figures," I thought as I shook my head.

I became even more wary after we were awakened in the middle of the night to the sound of screaming and cries for help. "What is going on now?" I wondered. That was when I found that the *Safari* Ants were invading our cabin and falling off the ceiling into our students' sleeping bags, biting hapless members of our group.

Later that morning when Steven responded nonchalantly to our ant problem, my fear that it would take a major disaster to prompt his concern was reinforced. He was a cross between Indiana Jones and Faulkner. I had a cautious admiration for his lifestyle, yet I found myself thinking: "How can anyone enjoy watching people suffer through so many physical hardships?"

After participating in a full day of mountaineering activities, my perspective changed dramatically. I saw my peers overcome resistance, conquer fear, and work together. I realized that all the exercises were designed to bring out leadership qualities and teach cooperation. We were becoming stronger.

As we neared the end of our Outward Bound experience, I again appraised Steven, only this time I thought, "What a fortunate man. It must be rewarding to watch people push their limits and break through and achieve a sense of high self-esteem, self-respect, and group unity." I will never forget Steven; he had a special quality that most people in authority lack. He had gained my personal respect.

Photo: Gary Bacon

Working with the Kibos

Jonathan Tourzan

Our students had been put into four patrols with the NYS the first night. We were given the names of four famous peaks in Kenya—Elgon, Nelian, Kenya, and Kibo. I was placed in the Kibo Patrol. Kibo was the highest peak in Kenya, so, as a member of Kibo Patrol, we had to strive to be the best. We were proud to be Kibos.

The Americans and Kenyans in our patrol quickly bonded during the activities. We always pushed each other to new limits. I specifically remember the ropes course as an example of this. I had come far but approached what seemed like an insurmountable obstacle. There was a shaky rope about ten feet long over a small pond. It connected to two ropes on the other side on which one could support oneself. With these two ropes, one could climb up to a ladder.

Twice I tried to make it across but fell in the water. Each time the members of my patrol cheered me on. They told me to try a third time. I quickly lost my balance crossing the rope, but, this time, I gathered up the strength to jump. I fell forward and grabbed on to the two ropes with both hands. Everyone cheered. I felt so good, as if I could do anything. The Kenyans told me that I was a soldier.

On the second evening Mwambui, a Kenyan Kibo, called me over and told me to come with him. It had been a hard day, and I thought we were going to go somewhere quiet to relax and talk. To my surprise, Mwambui took me behind the mess hall where there was a big truck piled high with wood. I went into the truck with Maurice, another Kibo, and two boys from other patrols whom I did not know. We passed out logs to other boys outside the truck who were making a big pile of wood behind the mess hall. We did this strenuous work for about half an hour. When I felt like stopping, they would encourage to continue. "You are a soldier," they would say, and this reaffirmation gave me the strength to push on when my fatigue made me feel like stopping.

After unloading the wood, I went to the bathroom to wash some clothes. One Kibo, Jeremiah, gave me some pointers on how to wash clothes properly. I explained that in America we had washing machines and did not wash by hand. He was amazed. Suddenly, the dinner bell rang. We had to run to make it on time; this time we arrived with smiles on our faces. That evening we sat around and talked. I told my new friends about education in America. They were fascinated. They told me about their tribes and homes. We got very close to one another. When it was time to go to bed, I said good-bye to my fellow Kibos. I went back to my cabin with a greater understanding of these young Kenyans, their values, and their ways. We had many differences, but we carried within a common spark of humanity that bonded us.

Preparing for the hike

Jonathan Tourzan

The next day, we went into Loitokitok to buy supplies for our excursion into the Maasai country. We bought *mabati* (sheets of metal roofing material) at a small hardware store. We also bought bananas, milk, and rice to eat, a gift of two hundred sodas for the Maasai, and small trees to plant with the Maasai in the village. We put these items in and on Steven's Land-Rover and returned to the Mountain School. It started to pour while we were in Loitokitok, sending everyone for cover, but it cleared up quickly. These unpredictable rains occurred often, and Steven was worried that these storms would make the hike difficult.

That evening after dinner, our Learning Community group had an emergency meeting in which we discussed whether every student should be permitted to go on the trip. Some students had not been keeping their commitment to the group to *fully participate in all events*. Some of us were concerned about their commitment level. It seemed that the process of maintaining a high level of commitment in a group was a never ending challenge.

After our stay at Outward Bound, we planned to hike into Maasai land and camp in a small village. Some people had concerns about whether we could all handle this activity. Some of our students had not participated in all the activities at Outward Bound; they had just sat and watched. One of our girls tried to stay in bed one day and not do anything; another attempted to go hide in our cabin. A small group of our students even went to Gary during our first morning of Outward Bound activities and demanded that we leave the school. Gary just gave a sympathetic look and said: "This is what we agreed to do. Now we are going to complete it."

Overcoming resistance
Andy Lipson

Steven McCormick had said that tomorrow's hike was physically possible for all, but he was not sure that our level of commitment was high enough for all of us to make it. The weather conditions were completely unpredictable, and, if some of us got too tired, too hot, or too wet on the hike, there would be no way we could turn back.

Steven, Gary, Jonathan, and some other students thought that a few of our group members had not demonstrated sufficient commitment to be permitted to go. I was not one of the students in question, but I wanted to be, so that I could have an easy way out. I talked about it with Paula, and we agreed that if anyone stayed behind we would stay with them. I was incredibly tired and wanted to have a relaxing day to sleep in rather than have another cross-cultural experience.

We met in our cabin and pushed all the bunks back against the wall to form a big circle. We were prepared for a lengthy interpersonal. Our meeting began, with everyone saying what he/she wanted to do. Audrey wanted to go, and other people did not want her to go; I wanted to stay, and they wanted me to go. We all agreed that we would have to make a firm commitment if the hike was going to work. After what seemed like hours of heated discussion, we decided that we would all go. I was the last person to give in. It was Ryan who finally convinced me to go. He told me: "If you don't go I will seriously lose respect for you! Here is an opportunity you probably will never have again, and you want to pass it up for an extra day to sleep in and do your laundry." I finally relented.

I was glad that I decided to go. I learned that when the going gets tough for me, I often want to give up. I was lucky to have someone there to push me to my limit. Now I know that I can keep going and maintain my commitments. My self-imposed limits do not have to run me.

Bidding farewell again
Jonathan Tourzan

Although the Outward Bound instructors did not require it, our group chose to start our final day with the traditional run-and-dip. This was an activity that most of our group had resisted vigorously on our first day. Now that our group had reconnected we wanted to push through all remaining resistance.

We ate breakfast for the last time with our friends from NYS. Then we attended the morning meeting and said farewell to our Kenyan friends from the NYS and OBS. Many students exchanged addresses with their new Kenyan friends. The moment was mixed with sadness and joyful anticipation as we went back to our cabins and packed our provisions for the trip into Maasailand.

Photo: Gary Bacon

CHAPTER 5: JOINING IN WITH THE MAASAI

We loaded our supplies onto Steven's Land-Rover. The jeep was quite a sight with *mabati* (roofing material) tied on top and the back packed full with food, tents, and sleeping bags. Steven was going to drive the Land-Rover all the way to the Maasai settlement on rough, dirt trails.

Hiking with the Morans
Jonathan Tourzan

The *matatus* picked up our group at the Outward Bound School. They drove us twenty-five miles over marginal dirt roads to a foot-trail that led to the Maasai settlement. Two young *morans* (Maasai warriors) were waiting there for us.

The morans had bright red clay on their heads and generous amounts of beaded jewelry, ranging from wristbands, to earrings and necklaces. They had come to lead us to their village and protect us from danger. Because lion attacks were a possibility in the area, the two warriors carried large spears that they handled astutely. Lions knew better than to cross the path of a *moran* because they were no match for these brave warriors. Kimani, the warden of the Outward Bound School, also accompanied us. Kimani spoke *Maa* (the language of the Maasai), *Kiswahili*, and English so he was a key communication link between us and the two *morans*.

The two *morans* were to escort us to their village. One walked in front of us, and the other walked behind us as we began our six-and-a-half mile trek across the plains. We were in a valley between Mt. Kilimanjaro and the Chyulu Hills. The soil was red and dry, and there were few trees. I noticed small hills located here and there as far as the eye could see. The day was very hot at first, but, as we neared the village, the sky darkened. When we were within sight of the village, it started to rain. The two *morans* were not particularly pleased about this development because the rain made the red ochre in their hair run. I had a raincoat, and I gave it to a *moran* to protect his hair from the downpour. He gave me a look of appreciation and friendship. At that moment, I felt that he recognized and accepted my humanness. Fortunately, the weather cleared up quickly.

Touching the land
Kelly McJunkin

I felt so close to the Earth as I walked; the great African plains stretched to the horizon in front of me; the historical Mt. Kilimanjaro rose behind me. The red soil was soft as I trekked to the Maasai school in my huge boots. Mountains rose to the sky on both sides of me. I breathed the warm air into my lungs; it had a deep, rich, earthy smell. Rain began to fall, sprinkling at first, and then pouring. I could feel each cool and refreshing drop touch my face. After the rain had muddied the topsoil, it stopped. The wet dirt collected on the bottom of my boots until it was hard to walk with the extra weight. I saw a small building in the distance; this was our destination, the Elangata-Enkima Primary School. We had finished our fifteen kilometer hike to the village.

The cool rain felt good after hiking six miles through the bush. The rain stopped as we approached the Maasai village, but the clouds reminded us that it could soon start again. When we arrived, some women and the headmaster of the school, Barnabas, greeted us. Steven McCormick, who had already arrived, instructed us to put up our tents.

Relating to the morans
Julie Paiva

When I heard that we were going to be camping in tents, I thought nothing of it. Yet putting up my green canvas tent next to a mud *boma*(hut) made me feel a little uncomfortable. It wasn't long before a group of *morans* came over to see who we were.

The *morans* are beautiful people. They are young men between the ages of fourteen and twenty-five who live in the bush. Traditionally they are warriors or hunters. The morans drape red and white cloth around themselves, and some wear rubber sandals made out of tires. They wear an abundance of colorful jewelry, made for them by prospective girlfriends, and paint their long, twisted hair with thick, red ochre (earth). They are very gentle but can be very powerful with the spears they carry.

When the *morans* came over to see our tents, they laughed. I showed them how to get inside through the zippers and layers of mosquito netting; they seemed intrigued. This was a wonderful introduction to interacting with the Maasai. Though I could not speak to them in their language, I spent hours communicating with them. We would just touch one another, admire each other's hair and clothes, and enjoy being in Maasailand together.

**Cooking in
the bush
Katy Arnovick**

By late afternoon, we had finished setting up our camp, so Julie and I set off to explore our new home. We referred to it as a village, yet it was not really a village. Two wood framed school buildings on the open plain near a circle of eight small huts does not feel like a village.

We wandered into one of the wooden buildings. It had dirt floors and about twenty hand-made wooden benches inside. Barnabas, the school master, told us that this was his classroom. On our way out, he mentioned that this was where we were going to cook dinner for our group shortly. Julie and I volunteered to do the cooking.

Dinner was to consist of a goat that we had purchased for the Maasai and some vegetables that we had bought in Loitokitok. We decided to begin preparing the dinner. This task turned out to be unexpectedly difficult. First, we had to decide what to make. We

Photo: Gary Bacon

had potatoes and rice and some soup base flavoring, so we decided to steam the rice and boil the potatoes. Even this was a much harder task than we had anticipated.

Rain clouds darkened the sky, and it wasn't long before we could hear rain pouring on the tin roof. We were cooking on two little gas burners, barely able to see our food in the dim light of our kerosene lantern. Then lightning started to flash. Julie got scared because she thought the metal roof might attract the lightning, so she left the room. I was still cooking over the fire; I felt hot. The lightning started getting worse; I was getting scared.

Julie came back into the room, having recovered from her fear. We finally finished the meal and placed it on one of the school benches for people to eat. It was not the tastiest meal I had ever made, but we all enjoyed it because we were so hungry.

I learned about preparing a group meal; I also got a chance to experience cooking without all the luxuries that we have at home, namely hot running water and a gas stove. This experience is one that I will never forget.

To celebrate our arrival in their village, the Maasai had planned a special feast in which a goat would be killed. I wanted to take part in all the Maasai festivities, but, being a vegetarian, I felt I could only eat the meat if I had a hand in killing the animal. Every time an individual eats meat, they are causing suffering to some living being. Because most people do not kill the animals that they eat, they are out of touch with this reality. If I were going to eat meat, I did not want to avoid witnessing the suffering experienced by the animal. In fact, I wanted to cause its suffering with my own hands. I asked Musa (Moses), a Maasai elder, if it would be all right for me to kill the goat. Musa appreciated my desire to be involved, and he readily agreed.

**Killing the goat
Jonathan
Tourzan**

Musa took me into a dark schoolroom. I saw the goat in the corner with a rope around its neck. Barnabas, the schoolmaster, held the animal tightly. Musa gave me a knife; I was scared. I kept asking whether it was time to start. Musa and Barnabas put tree branches and metal sheets on the ground to keep blood off the dirt floor. They also put a pot on the metal sheets to capture the blood from the goat's neck; the Maasai consider blood a delicacy and enjoy drinking it. Musa told me that it was time to start.

As I cut the goat's throat, its body writhed. I tried to kill with compassion, experiencing the suffering of the goat, letting its pain enter my heart. When I reached the artery at the back of the goat's neck, I felt the life start to leave its body. After Musa cracked its neck, its body went limp, and the goat died. Everything got so quiet in the room. I felt as if the goat were still there, still alive.

At this point, we began to butcher its warm body. I held one leg, and Musa pulled off the skin. After the skinning, we separated the organs. The Maasai use every part of the animal. Musa removed the raw kidney from the goat. He cut it into

---

four slices and gave pieces to Ryan, Andy, Gary, and me. The kidney was still warm from the kill. I had not eaten meat for almost a year. Shortly after eating the kidney, I left the room.

As I walked to the stream to wash my hands, I thought about what I had just done. I felt like I understood the process of dying in a deeper way. I also felt a great respect for all life. Plants and animals are all alive and must be killed to be eaten. Killing a goat made me conscious of this fact. I am now much more grateful for all the food I receive. The experience also confirmed my vegetarian beliefs, as taking the life of an animal is not a pleasant experience. As I washed my hands in the stream, I prayed for the goat. I offered it my love to give it the strength for its next incarnation.

Lighting the night
Jonathan
Tourzan

That evening we ate in the classroom. Students sat at the desks and ate stew. Several Maasai warriors had joined us for the evening. The Maasai would crouch together in groups around the open fire. They used an ingenious system of sticks to prop the goat quarters close to the fire to cook. When a quarter was cooked, a small group would gather around in the corner of the room and slice pieces for each other to eat. Some students did not want to go into the room where the goat was being prepared, so chunks of sizzling goat meat were brought to them in the other classroom. We also cooked enough *maize* (corn) over this fire to feed everyone.

There was a tremendous thunderstorm that evening. We were staying in a valley with Mt. Kilimanjaro on one side and the Chyulu Hills on the other. These two ranges caused the clouds to split over the village. On either side, lightning would explode from the clouds. This lightning was so intense that it would light up the sky, making it as bright as day. I had never seen such a spectacle in my life. Watching this awesome sight, I began to understand the respect that the Maasai have for the forces of nature that play such a prominent role in their harsh, but beautiful environment.

Imagine yourself in the middle of a great plain . . .
    pink lightning streaking the sky
You're in a smoke-filled mud hut
    in the center of this vast land.
Picture yourself crouched on all fours,
    curiously creeping toward a flaming bonfire.
Colorful Maasai warriors squat comfortably by the fire
    preparing their evening meal.
The dancing firelight fills the shadows and
    you capture a glimpse of their vibrant jewelry.
Their heads turn and their wild stares examine you,
    not sure what to think.
A vision collides with your thoughts . . .

Creeping toward the fire
Rebecca Sugg

A few days ago I had stepped off an aircraft onto the African continent. I had come from a place of high technology and microwave ovens to a place I had only seen in picture books and movies. In experiencing the planet earth, I realize how much substance my own land lacks and how these people blend in so well with their environment. The vision reminds me of a puzzle that I had put together long ago. I remember how it thrilled me that every piece fit just right.

The circle of warriors welcomed me in . . . they enjoy my presence. I ate with them and enjoyed being in their presence. I have much to learn about the Maasai people, and they have much to learn about me; thus, I began my journey through the Maasailand.

The next day began with a beautiful sunrise. We had an early breakfast of bread and *chai* (tea); then we cleaned the grounds around the school. Children started arriving at the school with their parents; everyone knew that we were going to have a special celebration on this day. People gathered around the school to begin the activities. At first our two groups were separate. We stood face to face and looked at each other bashfully. Gradually we began to interact and move closer together.

Experiencing joy
Jonathan Tourzan

The young children sang several traditional songs. Their innocent faces touched me greatly. Many of them had never been outside the region that encircled their village. After the songs, we split into four groups, each of which planted about six paper and jacarandas trees. We loosened the soil together, and then planted the saplings. On top of each tree, we put spiky branches to stop goats and cows from snacking on them. Each group then encircled the trees that they had planted and sang songs. I was touched by the happiness that such a simple act brought to these children. They all looked so content. I felt the same joy just being in their presence.

Connecting with children
Bruce Epis

I was filled with anticipation on the morning of our stay with the Maasai. After a breakfast of bread and tea, we visited the Maasai school. Barnabas, the head master, had started the school three years earlier. At first, he held class under a tree with only a few students and one textbook, which they had to share. Now, there are two wooden buildings, housing grades one through four.

I was struck by the beauty of the children and their bright smiles. They ranged in age from five to nine; they seemed intimidated by my height. They welcomed me by shaking my large hand with their tiny ones.

We worked with the small children to help them plant the trees that we had brought to their village. I helped dig a hole and then watched as a young boy carefully placed a drought-resistant jacaranda in the hole and covered it with soil. Then another child watered the saplings. Some of our students began singing Kenyan songs with the children in a circle around the trees. When my planting was done, I joined them.

It was a powerful and inspirational experience to see the singing children with snow-capped Mt. Kilimanjaro in the background. I breathed in the fresh, clear air. As I reflected on what we were doing, I realized that the trees that I had helped plant would remain and grow with the children and the school, long after our group had left.

I joined a small groups of Maasai children and Learning Community students. We carried our six small trees to a spot near one of the classrooms. We all helped to prepare the soil and to plant each tree. Two schoolboys took a large plastic container to the river and brought back water to pour over the

Planting for the future **Susan Abramson**

Photo: Laura Zarcone

newly planted trees. The teacher, Barnabas, assured us that he would assign students to tend each tree after our departure.

When we had planted the last tree, Barnabas named it the *Susan Tree* in my honor. A small boy shyly offered to be its caretaker.

After that, we stood in circles and sang many Maasai songs, clapping to the beat. One girl would sing a solo in the sweetest, purest tones that only a child's voice can make; then the others would join her, repeating the lines in a rich chorus.

I looked around at the faces of these young Maasai children and saw pride, courage, joy, hope, and goodness. I was so overcome by feelings of such strength that tears began streaming down my face. This moment will always stay with me.

**Sowing
friendship
Gary Bacon**

Maasai men, women, and children adorned in bright red, white, and blue clothing and jewelry came from their distant clusters of *bomas* to greet us. They came to welcome us with traditional songs and dances. They were preparing for the ceremony during which they would present gifts to each of our little band of twenty-four people.

We, too, were ready to join in the festivities with our own songs, dances, and gifts. We had brought two hundred bottles of orange and lemon sodas for the children. We had also brought *mabati* for roofing and paper trees to plant around the newly constructed school buildings.

The young Maasai children gathered about their older counterparts from the U.S. to begin the tree planting. Age and cultures blended in a swirl of activity; we broke the small saplings from the cardboard containers; we dug holes in the soft, rich earth, and we placed the young trees gently into their new home. While two students covered the roots with soil, another poured water from a big yellow bucket onto the freshly planted trees.

In a show of spontaneous celebration, Dana, Katy, and Rebecca joined hands and circled a newly planted tree. They began to chant harmoniously as they looked downward on what would someday be a shade tree for some yet unborn student of the Elangata-Enkima Primary School. This inspired a flurry of larger circles of students, young and old, who wished to celebrate the planting of these tiny trees.

Songs and chants of global music began to spring up around the small, newly constructed wooden school building. The strong voice of a seven year old girl pierced the air with song in her tribal tongue. This summoned a melodic response from all her classmates, resulting in a beautiful call and response tribute to the human spirit.

I moved about, feebly attempting to capture a piece of this magic in my camera's eye. Years of teaching and experience and inculturation and activity fell away. I was left only with the moment — naked and innocent and pure. Gone was my reference of past and future, and gone was my sense of *I*. What remained was the moment, unfiltered by comparison, contrast, or relativity.

Tears gushed from my eyes. The view through the camera lens blurred in a salten sea of bliss. All the students, black and white, and all the images of mountains and plains pooled into one. Life had achieved union in a sea of universal harmony.

After we had planted the trees, our group was given a tour of the surrounding *bomas* and farms. We began by walking through a nearby *boma*. A *boma* refers to a hut or a circular compound of huts surrounded by *kojo kidogos* (prickly thornbushes or "wait-a-bits"). *Kojo kidogos* earned their un-

Touring the bomas
Jonathan Tourzan

Photo: Gary Bacon

usual name by causing passer-bys who walked into them to wait-a-bit to get unhooked from their spiky branches. The Maasai use *kojo kidogos* to keep out lions during the night. If the lions are not kept out, they could have a feast of beef and goat, as the Maasai keep these beasts inside the *bomas* in the evening.

A *mama* (Maasai mother) showed me the inside of one mud hut. The huts seemed larger inside than they looked from the outside. They had a kitchen, a meeting room for guests, a bedroom, and a small room for keeping baby goats at night. The *boma* had about six huts, each inhabited by a different family in the community. The ingenuity of the whole organization of the *bomas* amazed me. They were constructed of mud, dung, and straw, yet they seemed to provide sturdy and comfortable, even pleasant, living quarters.

After seeing the *bomas*, we went out to the *shamba* (farms). We saw crops, such as *maize*, spinach, tomatoes, and cabbage. Traditionally the Maasai are nomadic herdsmen — the formation of game parks and the emphasis on agricultural development have restricted their movement, forcing some of them to settle down into one region. Finally, we walked down to the stream. This small stream brought irrigation to the region, making it ideal for human settlement.

During our tour, the school children walked with us. They would come up to me and inquisitively look into my eyes. When I gave one of them my hand, he smiled contentedly. We walked hand-in-hand to the stream. I was touched by the innocence of these children who had never seen the greed and cruelty of our Western world. Their world seemed to end at that stream and go no farther. After the tour, I went back to my tent where I played a raga on my flute for my little friends. This music was completely new to them, and they listened in awe. I felt good sharing this small part of myself with the beautiful children.

**Entering
the boma
Vanessa Tubbs**

A little boy grabbed my hand and led me to the entrance of a *boma*. *Kojo kidogos* surrounded the small compound to keep wild animals out. A circle of about six huts surrounded a six inch sea of fresh cow dung. Children ran around barefoot, ignoring the millions of flies. I wanted to take off my shoes and feel the dung squish between my toes.

One little boy yanked my hand, leading me to a hut. I had to duck down to fit inside. It was so dark that I couldn't see in front of me, but I could smell the wood from a burning fire. I worked my way through a maze-like passage to the main room. From the sunlight that crept through the cracks, I noticed two small rooms with bedding on the ground. Then I noticed a woman sitting by the fire, and she spoke to me in Maasai. I couldn't understand her, so I went to her and shook her hand. I greeted her in Maasai, "*Sopa!*" (Hello!). Then the boy tugged at my hand and led me out; I didn't want to go; I wanted to stay and learn more about this simple, yet wonderful way of life.

As we walked about the Maasai village, I met Maria; she was the cutest little five year old girl! She looked adorable in her little, well-worn red dress.

Making a new friend
Katy Arnovick

She looked different from the other children. There was something about the way she looked that attracted me when I first saw her. She had a wonderful, innocent look that came through her deep, dark brown eyes.

When I bent down to give her a piggy back ride, she climbed onto my back and gripped my shoulders with her tiny hands. I knew that in spirit we would always be together.

As I stepped into the classroom, I noticed the dirt floor, the small hand-made wooden benches, and the beautiful children who sat on them. Several children squeezed close to each other to share well used textbooks.

Teaching English
Vanessa Tubbs

Their teacher said, "It is good that you are here. You can help my students with their English." Then he busied himself with a small group of eager children. The children stayed on task without supervision and freely helped each other with their lessons.

I sat with two little girls and listened to them read slowly in English. They touched me deeply with their serious desire

Photo: Julie Paiva

---

to learn. I was only able to spend a short time with them that day, yet I can still close my eyes and hear their sweet voices.

Sharing gifts of love
Leah Mowery

I sat on a rock in front of my tent in Maasai land. The sky was gray and cloudy, and the air was hot and wet from the rain that fell throughout the day. The land stretched out in all directions, with only small hills to upset the plain. I wore my *kanga*, a wrap-around skirt worn in Kenya, and hiking boots borrowed from the Outward Bound school. I felt clunky and immobile; I even felt awkward crossing my legs.

I had a string bracelet attached to my *kanga* by a safety pin. We heard that the Maasai were going to be giving us jewelry as presents. This motivated Ian and a few of us to weave friendship bracelets to give in return.

People were standing around me, and two Maasai *morans* were communicating in *Kiswahili*. As I worked on the bracelet, I thought about how I used to make them with my friends; here I was with the Maasai, making these same bracelets. A few Maasai would even be wearing them, just as some of my friends did.

During the *baraza* (party), we were standing in a circle of about 350 Maasai. Everyone from the surrounding *bomas* had come to see us and to welcome us. A *mama* entered the circle with a basket of jewelry. She would select an appropriate piece and put it on one of us, sometimes with the help of another *mama*. Musa explained to us the significance of each colorful piece of jewelry. I received an oval earring that was half a foot long. It was made out of leather and beaded on the front. It was too big for my ear, so they put it on a beaded string for me to wear around my neck.

I wanted to pass the jewelry that I had made on to someone, so I went to Musa and asked him to whom I should give it. He led me to the side of the circle where more women sat and spoke to them in Maasai. Then he lifted one woman's arm and told me that I could give it to her. As I tied the green and blue bracelet onto her wrist, my hands were shaking; I feared that I wouldn't be able to get the knot tied. I didn't know what she thought of the present. She made some comment to her companions, but I couldn't understand what it was. She had been smiling the whole time, but I was not sure if she enjoyed it.

I didn't know to whom I should give the other bracelet. I didn't know any of the women, and Musa had left me long ago and was with other members of my class. I looked at the women and got smiles in return, but nothing led me to a particular person.

Photo: Audrey Bethke

I saw Susan near me talking to an old *mama*. I asked her if she had any ideas about giving the other bracelet. Susan looked down at the old woman with love and respect. Susan said, "If I were to tell you who I thought should get it, it would have to be this *mama*. She is a special woman."

I followed her advice, and, as I was tying it on, I felt like I was paying a compliment to a very important person. I got the feeling that this woman was respected by her community and that she was a woman of great knowledge. I felt honored knowing that she would wear something that I had made. I hoped that she would remember me and this day with love and treat the present with care.

A group of young warriors stood in a circle, chanting and dancing. These *morans* form a special group within society. Most adult males have been warriors earlier in their lives, and they are proud of this heritage. The elders are also proud of the young *morans* who carry on the ancient tradition. I was struck by their pride and dignity as they stood together during the ritual.

Two groups of Maasai women sang songs; one group sang traditional tribal songs and the other group sang Christian songs. There has been a strong effort to convert the Maasai to Christianity as they are a rare group of people who still practice tribal religions. Several people asked me if our group were there to preach, as most whites who visit the village are missionaries. In contrast, our group performed a Sufi dance for the Maasai. The Maasai found this particularly interesting as they had never seen this type of dancing.

Photo: Steven McCormick

We then gave our presents to the Maasai. We brought them the roofing for their school and gave them sodas to drink. These sodas were a rare treat for the Maasai who seldom get into Loitokitok where sodas can be purchased. Each of our students received a colorful piece of jewelry made by the Maasai. I received a red and green Maasai warrior's necklace. Several speeches followed from Gary, Barnabas, Musa, Fiona, Vanessa, and me. One common theme of the speeches was the unity of all people on the planet. I realized that, although we are different colors, we are all children of God. Speeches were translated from English to Maasai, and from Maasai to English, so that everyone could understand.

I was standing at the edge of a circle of 350 happy, colorful Maasais with members of our group spread throughout. Gary was at the center presenting gifts on our group's behalf to the senior elders of the tribe. We gave them trees for shade, *mabati* for their school, and a five hundred dollar gift toward the construction of a new classroom.

Exchanging gratitude
Jenelle Flaherty

Musa, the Maasai who had arranged our visit, translated the elder's thankful words into English for us. Jon, Fiona, Laura, and Kelly carried the *mabati* into the circle on their shoulders. A group of elders sitting close to Rebecca and me clapped to show their thanks.

One of them turned to Rebecca and looked at her with deep gratitude and respect; he then spit on the ground in front of her, and turned back to the center of the circle to enjoy the rest of the ceremonies.

Rebecca and I stood there confused, wondering what the elder meant by spitting in front of her. Later I talked with Steven McCormick about it. He explained to me that some Kenyans, especially Maasai, have a custom of spitting at one's feet to show their gratitude. I felt good knowing that the Maasai people respected and appreciated our gifts, although I still felt strange about the spitting.

I was intrigued by the Maasai. They were dramatically different from any people I had ever seen. We stayed in their village for one night. On our second day the Maasai held a *baraza* during which we exchanged gifts. While we were presenting them with building materials for their school, a Maasai elder spit at my feet. I felt shocked at first; later I was told that, in their culture, when one spits at a person's foot, it symbolizes great respect.

Greeting one another
Rebecca Sugg

Joining in with the Maasai

I felt warm inside and I almost cried, knowing that we were representing our country in the best way we knew how. I think that both our groups will remember this experience forever.

Pausing to refresh
Fiona Hollins

I grabbed a bottle of cola from the crates that we had brought from Loitokitok. I handed a Maasai elder a soda and smiled shyly. He nodded and grinned to me in return. Taking a soda for myself, I crouched down next to him. We did not talk, but we looked at each other between sips. I thought about our different lifestyles and backgrounds; I realized that our differences did not matter. As we enjoyed each other's company and smiled at each other, I felt very close to him. Here we were, an American teen-age girl from Los Altos Hills, and a Maasai elder, who lived in a mud and dung hut, drinking sodas together in the hot African sun.

Experiencing the ritual
Jesse Baumgartner

As I came closer to the Maasai warriors, their power intensified. I took the smoothly carved stick that Musa handed to me and filled myself with a deep breath. Andy, Jonathan, Ian, and I, joined the morans in a rhythmic dance of power. The sun stung my back as I thrust my feet into the red soil. The warriors sang so deeply that I felt that they were channeling music from within the earth. I felt raw, at one with the land and its people.

Jumping with the morans
Jonathan Tourzan

The young warriors were doing a traditional dance with jumping and chanting to celebrate the *baraza*. This same dance gives the warriors the courage necessary to kill a lion, part of the Maasai rite of passage into manhood. After initiation, the *morans* continue to do the dance on festive occasions. Our visit and the resulting *baraza* created such an occasion, and a dozen *morans* gathered to sing and dance for us.

Musa approached Andy and me. He offered us the opportunity to join in; then he gave us ceremonial sticks. All the warriors carry smooth sticks as signs of power. We joined the circle and began chanting. The warriors were singing and moving their heads up and down to the pulsing rhythm. They encouraged me with friendly laughter and looks of approval.

Photo: Katy Arnovick

Each dancer took turns going into the middle of the circle and jumping. When my turn came, I was a little nervous. As I stepped into the circle, my bashfulness disappeared. Three times I jumped into the air. My mind felt as vast as the sky. After my final jump, I thumped my feet onto the ground and returned to the circle.

Leaning against my fellow dancers, I felt like a Maasai warrior. I knew how fortunate I was to receive this opportunity to participate directly in their traditional culture.

Understanding morans
Leah Mowery

The tent encloses me in hot, sticky air, so I unzip the tent and get out. In front of me are three Maasai men, standing and talking together in their native tongue.

They have a unique shape to their bodies, as if the wind on the plains and the harsh conditions of the sun shaped their bones. Their bodies are strong from the intense work that nomadic life demands; they seem to stretch toward the sky. Crimson cloth drapes over their shoulders and hangs below their waist. This covers their torso much like a robe. The men lean on walking sticks that appear to become extensions of their bodies. They walk with pride and dignity. Their steps connect with the land in a most spiritual way. The red ochre clay in their hair connects them even more to the land on which they live in such harmony.

Behind them, the peaks of Mt. Kilimanjaro rise out of an expanse of land that seems to go on forever. Around it are gray clouds, clouds quite different from those at home. They are strong and sharply defined. I imagine what it would be like to live with such beauty every day. I imagine this beauty surrounding the Maasai's unconscious spirit, dripping in and making them whole. Unlike so many people in my community that are detached from their environment, the *morans* live in close relation to everything around them. They know how to work with the world around them.

Departing in the rain

Jonathan Tourzan

After the party, we took down our tents and packed our gear into Steven's Land-Rover; Steven then went ahead on a different route. We left the village followed by several children. The plan was to meet Steven and the *matatus* on the other side of a nearby stream; this plan did not work out. Rain was falling very hard as we walked, making the roads very slippery. As a result, our vehicles had not arrived to meet us. The rain stopped shortly after we had crossed the river where the young children said good-bye to our group. Then we started the long walk to find the vehicles which we found stuck in the mud.

After we *rendezvoused* with the vehicles, getting back to Loitokitok turned out to be most difficult. The *matatus* got stuck at every turn on the road. Time after time our whole group had to get out and push them out of the mud; sometimes we needed Steven's Land-Rover to help us. We were most concerned when everyone, including the Land-Rover, got stuck at the same time. Tired and very muddy, we arrived at the Outward Bound School after dark. We were all exhausted from our exciting adventures in the Maasailand.

It was dark by the time we arrived at our destination at the Outward Bound Mountain School in Loitokitok. We were tired from our exciting adventure into the Maasailand, and wet and muddy from our arduous adventure back out. Everyone had helped and worked together that last day; no one had complained about the mud and rain. We had attained a heightened sense of unity; our group had matured and was functioning as one.

We went to bed tired, yet we knew that our objectives for this trip had been met. Soon we would be headed back home.

Realizing our objectives
Gary Bacon

Photo: Gary Bacon

CHAPTER 6: REFLECTING ON THE JOURNEY

The next morning before returning to Nairobi, we had plenty of cleaning up to do at the Outward Bound compound. Several students had borrowed hiking boots from the school, and we had to scrape thick layers of mud off of them. We had to clean our dormitory where the floor had gotten extremely dirty from the trackings of forty-two muddy feet. We had finished our cleaning jobs by late morning. We put our baggage into our *matatus* and said farewell to the people at the Outward Bound Mountain School.

Rounding it out
Jonathan
Tourzan

After a six-hour drive, we arrived back at the YMCA in Nairobi. We finally had a few hours of free time to relax. That evening, some students went to an African disco, where they danced with their Nairobi homestay families until late in the evening. The club's patrons were mostly local black Africans. We felt welcomed as we danced to the music of the Gnats, a popular African band from Zaire.

The next day was our last in Kenya, and we spent most of it shopping. Our first stop was the Jua Kali metal workers market. The clanging sounds of men hammering discarded tin cans into pots, pans, and clothing chests filled this lively market. The market was a classic example of recycling; seemingly useless objects were transformed into new and highly practical items.

From the metal market, we went to several other specialty shops. One shop sold clothing and scarves. A second shop sold exquisite hand crafted wood carvings. A third shop sold tribal crafts, such as drums, spears, and ebony carvings. Our group made like tourists and bought all sorts of interesting items. After visiting these shops, we went to the large downtown market where we purchased baskets, jewelry, and other native crafts.

After our shopping, we drove to the home of Karen Blixen, the woman whose life inspired the novel *Out of Africa*. Her home is a major tourist attraction, and several vans filled with tourists were waiting to take a tour. We decided that we did not want to spend our last afternoon in Kenya in a crowd of white tourists; our direct cultural experience had resulted in our identifying more with the African culture.

Then we drove to the crest of the Ngong Hills where we had a spectacular view of the Rift Valley. A colorful Kenyan sunset lighted up the sky during this last evening. It would be the last time that we saw the sun setting in this far-off land.

Getting an overview
Jenelle Flaherty

What an incredible sight for our last evening in Kenya! The *matatus* drove us to the top of the Ngong hills, the highest point of land as far as the eye could see. I felt so expanded.

I stood in waist-high grass on the side of the tallest peak. To one side, I could see the lights of Nairobi and, on the other, the vastness of the Rift Valley. The lights of Nairobi seemed to spread out for miles, and the Rift valley stretched endlessly toward the distant horizon.

As I gazed across the Rift Valley, I was absorbed by its enormous presence. It spread out before me, reflecting the muted evening light, untainted by the glimmer of the city lights. The clouds above Nairobi cast a gray shadow over the city. Colors of peach, purple, and blue outlined the white clouds, highlighting the beauty of the Rift Valley. As my eyes passed over the denseness of Nairobi and the openness of the Rift Valley, I bid my last farewell to Kenya.

That night, we had a special dinner at the Carnivore Restaurant. This restaurant is famous for the wide varieties of meat offered to its customers. Such delicacies as zebra, giraffe, and wildebeest are cooked over a fire and brought to the hungry customer. Our group provided quite a contrast with half of us eating from the vegetarian menu and the other half eating exotic meats.

Bidding farewell
Jonathan
Tourzan

After leaving the restaurant, we went directly to the Nairobi Airport. Maina and Julius stayed with us until we passed customs where they sadly bid us farewell.

As I passed through the check-in gate, I thought about the many new friends whom I was leaving behind. I had seen so much of this beautiful country. Yet I realized that there was even more that I had not seen. I had been through the experience of a lifetime, one that I would never forget.

Upon arriving back home in the U.S., I try to reflect. It is hard for me to say just how my Kenya experience and the friends I made there have affected me. My process of change has been such a deep, internal one. I know that years from now I will notice a new character trait in myself and wonder where it came from, and then I will remember: "Oh yeah, that comes from a lesson I learned in Kenya!"

Seeing with
new eyes
Leah Mowery

Yet, there are some changes and insights that are obvious to me now. I see my community and the people around me more clearly. I am struck by the tremendous lack of connection in this country. I feel that I have lost a sense of where I belong in my community. I feel that our country has become lost in its search for individualism.

I am afraid that Kenya may be in danger of falling into the same trap. I see that when people move from a well-connected tribal life to a fragmented urban life that they can lose touch with a special inner quality. This is happening in Nairobi as its population soars. Now I realize that this has been the case in many communities in the U.S. for many decades. When people lose touch with their roots, they are less sure to whom they can turn in time of need. This can create a social climate of low self-esteem, abusive family life, or drug abuse. Somehow, I cannot picture people murdering one another or becoming addicted to cocaine in a close-knit tribal community. People are too supportive and aware to let this happen.

It is so easy for people to slip through the cracks in such a huge society. After living in the bare material conditions of Kenya, I feel closer to the people I see on the street of this country. I realize just how human they really are, and I wonder if they feel lost at all. I see that people have lost touch with basic human needs like taking care of the environment, being of service to others, working toward spiritual values. We seemed to have lost the sense that we are all connected, that the pain of another is also our own pain. In Kenya I experienced the deep connection that the Maasai have with everything around them, and, through this experience, I am able to find that place in me.

I walk down the street in my community and want to greet everyone whom I see, but we all seem to be tied to separate realities. We are so afraid to show our inner-selves to each other. While in Kenya, I felt that people opened to me and didn't have anything to hide.

Yes, I am also very fortunate to live in the U.S.. I do not have to pay to get a good education, and I am assured of going to college. I will get a reasonably well-paying job when I finish my studies. I am also blessed with being around different points of view and numerous ethnic cultures with which I can experiment.

I am not stuck in a situation from which I cannot escape like some of my friends in Kenya. My Nairobi brother did not like living in the city, but it was the only place where he could get a job. My Nairobi sister had to wait a year after college before she could get a job, in spite of her being bright and well educated.

The Kenya experience taught me about myself. Before I left, I was caught up in many thoughts and feelings, and I had trouble expressing them to others. If I were angry, I would let my feelings sit; then I would twist myself into knots.

In Kenya I was always pulled out of myself; the situation demanded that I participate. I could not go into my reaction patterns because I saw that they were not effective. I was cast into so many new situations and had to make them work without relying on the usual conveniences. I learned to deal with things as they came and didn't get stuck in the details of what I did not have. Now, material comforts and money do not seem as important to me. I know that I can enjoy many things without money, such as hiking, biking with my friends, gardening, cooking for people. These things make me happy. I do not need the luxuries, such as cars and expensive clothes, that I thought I needed. These things seem unnecessary now because I have experienced living without them.

I am better at accepting people for who they are; I do not get stuck on the details of their character. I feel better about myself because everyone accepted me completely in Kenya. I'm not so worried about my outside appearance because there is something more important inside that is expressed through human interaction and caring.

After entertaining this long swirl of ideas, I still have to wonder if I have *really* changed. Is there some deeper part of me that has been so affected, so shaken, that my life pattern is altered permanently? Did my belief system swing sharply, sending me in a completely different direction? I know that something happened, yet it is too early for me to fully comprehend it.

Colonizing the mind
Laura Zarcone

When I think of African history, I think of the exploitation by Germany, France, England, Italy, Holland, Spain, and Portugal. I have little conception of Africa before colonization. While visiting Kenya, I saw first hand some of the after-effects of colonization.

While I was waiting in Kandara for the matatu to take us to our rural homestays, the villagers stared at me intensely; I wondered why. Later, I realized that the Kenyans were staring because of the color of my skin. My skin color represented the actions that had been carried out by people of my color. Until 1963, the British ruled Kenya. While in power, they seized the best land in the Kenyan highlands. When the people objected, tens of thousands of Kenyans were killed or forced to relocate. So the inhabitants of the highland community of Kandara had every right to stare, to be suspicious of white people. Sadly enough, because of our color, we represented the oppressors of the past. To the Kenyans' credit, once we interacted with them, all the negative feelings disappeared. We were left with a sense of understanding for the people and their vastly different culture.

Colonization also contributes to environmental problems. A Third World country which has been exploited for seventy-five years, and then becomes independent, is often far behind other nations economically; consequently, the environment is the last issue on the agenda of these nations. Standard of living, consolidation of power, illiteracy, and health problems receive greater attention.

Often such countries turn to the technology of the West in an attempt to modernize. This approach often extracts a high price from the environment. In the Muranga District, we were shown rivers that had been contaminated by pesticides. In Nairobi, I saw waste sites where toxins were simply dumped onto the earth. The West has set a bad precedent for developing nations. In our First World quest for comfort, we have failed to see how our ways are damaging. Unfortunately, countries like Kenya that are trying so hard to develop and progress, often follow our ecologically unsound examples.

When traveling with people, as in camping, one can quickly become aware of one another's strengths and weaknesses; this was true in traveling with the Learning Community. I became bonded with this group. These students are all very precious to me. I watched them go through many experiences, ranging from fatigue on the airplane trip to *Safari* Ants in their bunks in the middle of the night. These experiences stretched their physical and mental endurance.

Bonding with the group
Susan Abramson

I will always remember these special moments: Gary talking to the students — sometimes they listened and sometimes not; Jonathan killing the goat and playing with the children; Vanessa filming and smiling and ready for anything; Fiona's easy, flowing acceptance of things and her friendship with Alice; Jenelle saying, "I can't" and then doing it anyway; Kelly speaking her mind; Jon being so sick, but getting up and hiking to the Maasai village anyway; Rebecca sitting in the van on the way to the Maasai, eating three chocolate bars reading *Tommyknockers*; Katy, Rebecca, Dana, and Julie singing the melodies from twenty years of sitcoms while sitting in the dark van on the way to the Carnivore Restaurant; Bruce bringing balloons to the Muranga children and walking into the riot; Andy stepping into the sump hole at the market; Jonathan and Andy jumping with the Maasai morans.

I will also remember when I lay in the room in Muranga with Dana, Paula, Megan, and Laura, waiting three hours for the van to take us back to Nairobi; Ian smiling and looking so happy; Jesse looking at the van stuck in the mud and shaking his head; Heather, on the ground, buttering twelve loaves of bread, with her scarf on her head; Katy cooking in the Maasai kitchen; Audrey resolving to go on the hike; Ryan swimming with the Kenyan students; Leah, the first one helping to push the van out of the mud; Laura, the first one climbing the wall at Outward Bound.

A strong bond formed between us as well. I never laughed so hard as I did with Joyce and Gary. When Joyce and I realized that we had to walk two miles to the Post Office and lick stamps for 750 postcards in two hours, we laughed helplessly until we cried. Sorry, students, but when Gary, Joyce, and I found out about the *Safari* Ants, we were on the floor.

I admire Gary for his humor and steadfastness in difficult situations. How often did we hear him respond to our complaints of not having this or that, by reminding us that "It was on the list." I admire Gary for his leadership and vision. He held his vision for Kenya when he faced students' defeats and parents' fears. He always believed in his vision, and he, perhaps more than anyone, made it happen. He put himself on the line with the students, parents, and school administration. He has always worked hard for students in order for the Learning Community to succeed.

Photo: Gary Bacon

I admire Joyce for being the bad guy, giving all the shots, putting up with all the fears and complaints. Then, later, she became the good guy, helping the sick and weary with her nursing skills. I admire Joyce for her sense of humor, her coolness under pressure, and her willingness to put up with untold discomforts even though she admits, "I'm not a camper."

Our group camaraderie impressed me the most. Our way was the easy, natural way that people can be when they share the day-to-day experiences of living. I think that these students in the Learning Community are very fortunate to have this kind of relationship with each other. As I reflect on our journey to Africa, I think that it may take us several years to assimilate and appreciate what we experienced together.

Kenya –
I remember warm, fragrant air,
Smiling, singing children,
Friendships with the Elgon Patrol
    at the Outward Bound School,
Working in the corn fields
    with my Muranga host family,
Tree-planting and dancing with the Maasai,
I'll always cherish these wonderful
    memories of Kenya.

**Connecting
as one
Fiona Hollins**

Our trip holds so much meaning for me because I helped organize it. We all encouraged each other to contribute as much as possible to our group efforts of fund-raising, research, and dedication in order to make our trip joyful, rewarding, and educational. I know that we met the goals that we developed for ourselves at the beginning of the year.

We learned about the Kenyan way of life by living with host families. We learned about social and environmental issues through observation, through talking to people, and through our involvement in service work. We helped create a sense of global unity, another of our goals, by developing close relationships with the many people we met. Through our slide presentations to people back home and through our contributions to our service projects, we are contributing to the creation of a better world.

This was the first time I have lived in a Third World country. Now that I am back in the United States, I am much more aware of the luxury and opportunity that I have here. Yet, I no longer see vast differences between the United States and Kenya. I have learned that, whether we are affluent white Americans or developing Black Kenyans, we are all humans, and we can learn from each other's differences.

My stay in Kenya helped me to see the world as smaller. We transcended barriers of speech, race, and upbringing to form special, caring relationships with people of diverse cultures. My direct experience—in a joyful connection between two peoples from opposite sides of the earth—proved to me that peaceful relations between different cultures are entirely possible.

Afterthought

Our students began the year by asking fundamental questions concerning their education. They wished to know themselves better; they wanted to relate together more effectively; they wanted to know what they could study in the world; and they wanted to know how to make a difference. Although a progressive change did occur in the orientation of this group, they did not abandon these basic questions as they developed their cultural exchange to Kenya.

As an educator, I have been trained to look for a change in the learner. Without change, we conclude that learning did not take place. In my ten years as a traditional educator, I spent most of my time passing on information and testing for its retention. Undoubtedly, this time-honored process will continue to be important in education. Yet, in my last twenty years as an educator, I have been challenged to look for more. I have come to see other, more important, outcomes.

Education, in my view, must not only instruct the learner in the highest achievements of the culture but also awaken the learner to see higher possibilities. It must liberate the learner to aspire to and become something greater.

The Learning Community students' quest for self-understanding was transformed by their experience. They created a vision of the world in which they were an integral part. They were co-creators of reality in their new world view. Their question "Who am I?" grew to take on a collective spirit. This happened many times in many ways — in Nairobi, in Kandara, in Loitokitok, in Elangata-Enkima — as they became one with their brothers and sisters on the other side of the world. Transformation of individual consciousness gave rise to collective consciousness. Their fundamental nature began to change in a dramatic way.

The nature of the group experience also changed. As the students worked on their relationships with each other and learned how to communicate more honestly and more directly, they transcended another basic question. "How can we relate better?" became "How can we work together to promote peace and understanding in the world?".

The concept of service was transformed into a higher form for this group, too. Some members started with a limited view of service. They stated that they would not go on to Kenya unless they were constantly working in service to poor people or to the land. This one-sided view became transformed into a desire to be with, learn from, assist, and be assisted. They grew to seek an interrelationship with the people they met, one that was mutually beneficial and resulted in a sense of unity. It was an experience in which everyone involved received a larger gift.

Stages in the transformation of this group occurred before, during, and after our journey to Kenya. The community building experiences that we shared prepared us; the journey became our tempering fire; the writing project and the ongoing integration process shaped the final form.

The preparatory stages were profound. Before beginning the year, we invited students to join us who were willing to make a high commitment. We wanted to give young people, who had a desire for self improvement and an openness for new experience, a chance to work together.

We spent hours in communication sessions. We learned about our strengths and weaknesses; we acknowledged our joys and fears. We shared how we saw one another and how we felt about one another. Sometimes this was painful; more often it felt liberating and joyful. Our honesty enabled us to become more accountable.

The expressions *personal responsibility* and *integrity* came into use in our group. The freedom from old behaviors and old beliefs, which comes from introspection, enabled our group to take charge at both the personal and collective levels. *Empowerment* became the watch-word.

As we developed more healthy interpersonal relationships, our group energy rose. It was easier to challenge our group members' behaviors, support their growth, and celebrate their accomplishments. Having accomplished these fundamental levels of group development, we had a foundation upon which we could work. We became a creative, cooperative team committed to the success of the entire group.

Only then could we direct the group's initiative and collectively take charge. We formulated group goals and objectives and began to plan and to develop activities in the world through which we could achieve our goals. The process of implementation gave us a sense of purpose and helped us to learn the value of inquiry and networking.

Of course, we also had to develop mechanisms for ensuring that students kept their agreements and completed their assignments. The process was not easy; it required hard work, yet in the end, it was well worth it.

Periodically, we took time to reflect on our progress and to evaluate group and individual performance. The cycle of goal setting, planning, action, reflection, and evaluation led us to the completion of our projects. We made time to acknowledge and to appreciate one another's growth and achievement. We sought to bring this spirit of celebration into our daily work. Love manifested itself, in part, in the celebrative nature of our community.

It is too early to know what effect this experience will have on our students' lives. Still, the decisions and choices that they have made in the short span of time since our year together, seem to be in alignment with the values we worked so hard to cultivate. Their current choices, which have become their current life experiences, will ultimately shape their future.

Some of our group are still in high school; although most have graduated and are currently enrolled in colleges. We offer the following short sketches of our students' current situations as indicators of the lasting effect of our work together.

Katy Arnovick is attending Oak Grove High School, a small private, international school in Ojai, California. The school is based on the teachings of the

Indian philosopher Krishnamurti. She and her classmates already have traveled to the southwest U.S. to study American Indian culture and anthropology.

Jesse Baumgartner, Jon Rinard, Leah Mowery, and **Heather Hoppas** have returned to The Learning Community for the academic year. As the second year's core group, they provide continuity from the previous year's experiences and lessons. They also provide leadership for the group's next venture.

Audrey Bethke is attending De Anza College in Cupertino, California and plans to complete her studies at the University of California. She chose to major in Psychology because of her strong interest in working with people and in understanding their behavior. She also has shown a keen interest in photography and has publicly exhibited her Kenya photos.

Bruce Epis and **Andy Lipson** are continuing their studies in the standard curricular track at LAHS. Bruce will complete his studies through the American Field Service in France next year. Andy is strengthening his interest in medical illustrations.

Jenelle Flaherty found travel exciting so, upon graduation, she spent a week in central Mexico. After that she moved to Mt. Shasta, California, to experience personal independence and country-living.

Fiona Hollins is attending innovative Hampshire College in Massachusetts. She says that travel helped make the world smaller for her; now, she sees herself as part of the world. Her studies in psychology and nutrition have even taken a global perspective. She also is researching social change through non-violence.

Dana Jensen is attending Butte County Junior College in Chico, California. She is considering majors in Anthropology or World Cultures.

Ann Kaye is attending Foothill Community College in Los Altos, California, majoring in Business and Psychology. She overcame her aversion to flying by traveling to Mexico after graduation with some of her classmates.

Adam Lipson is attending California State University in San Francisco. Besides his general studies, Adam is studying Film Production and English with a strong vocational interest in script writing, especially for film.

Ryan Marton is also attending California State University in San Francisco. Ryan is considering a sociology major and is creating an urban-life video in which his interest in sociology can be explored. He attributes his motivation in college to our program.

Megan Mathias is attending De Anza Community College in Cupertino, California. She is majoring in the Administration of Justice with the goal of becoming an attorney. To round out her studies at De Anza, she will travel to Italy later this year to study Art for one quarter.

Kelly McJunkin is taking a year off from school before pursuing further academic study. She is saving her money to fund a return trip to Kenya later this year to visit her homestay families. She says her trip to Kenya helped her to become more environmentally aware.

Julie Paiva attended Foothill Community College for one quarter, then transferred to the University of California, Davis. Her study emphasis at the University is Foreign Studies, with a declared major in Anthropology—because of the Kenya trip. Julie says, "After traveling to Kenya, I want to go everywhere!"

Ian Perkins is completing his high school education in Appleton, Wisconsin, where his father has accepted a teaching position at Lawrence College.

Rebecca Sugg is completing her high school studies at Menlo-Atherton High School in Atherton, California. She plans to attend the University of Oregon in the coming year to major in Psychology.

Jonathan Tourzan is attending the University of California, Berkeley, majoring in Asian Studies. He already has plans to major in economics in graduate school. Jonathan was one of eight U. S. high school students to be selected to receive a national award for service this year—due, in part, to his participation in our Kenyan service projects.

Vanessa Tubbs is attending De Anza Community College in Cupertino, California. Last year she led us in learning Kenyan songs; now, she is majoring in drama and music. She has been in two plays this year, including a service-oriented dramatic production designed to raise consciousness about the AIDS disease.

Paula Wright is completing her high school in an independent learning program in the Chico, California.

Laura Zarcone has been on a six month, self-initiated tour of eastern and western Europe. Her travels also led her back to Africa to visit the Ivory Coast. While in Norway, she studied the unique social structure of the Lapps in preparation for her academic studies when she returns home. She has applied to the Independent Studies Program at the University of California, Santa Cruz.

These students left a legacy of love in Kenya through the personal friendships they made. They also left lasting goodwill in the service projects that they funded after the trip. Our group was able to raise $5000 more than the actual expenses. We decided to allot this reserve to service projects we had researched while in Kenya.

Before our departure, we purchased more than twenty pair of new soccer shoes for Father Grol's Undugu Society boys. Upon our return, we made a monetary contribution to the Society. We also donated money to IDEX and World Neighbors, two organizations that fund and assist development projects in Kenya.

We wished to make our money available to an individual, a school, and a community. We provided our young Kenyan friend Alice a scholarship to attend high school. We donated enough money to complete the construction of a medical dispensary in our Kikuyu homestay community. We also funded the construction of classrooms in the Maasai village that we visited. The trees we planted in Maasailand will provide shade for future students of the school.

We were also the beneficiaries. We were privileged to go out into the world and challenge our basic beliefs and assumptions. We were able to take an open, inquisitive spirit into the world and return with a new global vision.

Most importantly, we were able to embrace and be embraced by people of another culture — physically, emotionally, culturally, and spiritually. In the process, we were able to feel the deep connection of the human spirit. Our connections transcended the boundaries between people, cultures, races, and hemispheres. We had set upon a path to Kenya and, ultimately, took a journey that led back to our own hearts.

Gary Bacon, Ph. D.
The Learning Community
December 18, 1990

Glossary

asante sana (S) - an expression of appreciation meaning *thank you very much.*

askari (S) - soldier.

baba (S) - father, often used in conjunction with the name of a man's eldest son, e. g. Baba Maina.

baraza (S) - a celebration or party.

boma (M) - a small dung hut housing a family; usually part of a circle of huts, or kraal, surrounded by thorny bushes.

bwana (S) - mister, as in "Jambo bwana."

chai (S) - tea, a daily drink throughout the country.

chapati (S) - fried white-flowered bread.

duka (S) - a shop or store.

habari gani (S) - a common greeting asking the question "What's new?"

hakuna matata (S) - an expression assuring that *there are no problems.*

harambee (S) - working together as a community to achieve common ends. Literally: pulling together. This concept was introduced by Jomo Kenyatta, first president of Kenya in 1963, to rally his people to work together toward Kenya's development.

hotel (S) - a place to eat, a restaurant.

jambo (S) - a common greeting meaning *hello* or asking "How do you do?"

kanga (S) - a piece of clothe often used as a wrap-around shirt.

karibuni (S) - welcome, as in *welcome to my home.*

A reader's guide to Kenyan terms and expressions:

The accompanying list of terms was used in creating this publication. The letter following each word denotes its tribal or regional origin— (S) Swahili, (M) Maasai, and (K) Kikuyu.

Kenya nchi nzuri (S) - an expression meaning *Kenya is a beautiful country.*

Kikuyu (K) - a tribe originating in the fertile, central highlands of Kenya.

Kiswahili (S) - a common language of the people of East Africa, drawing largely from Bantu tribal languages and Arabic, with some English. Literal meaning: the language of the people of the coast. The official language of Kenya, although English is taught in the schools and spoken by most Kenyans.

kojo kidogos (S) - thorny bushes. Literally, *wait-a-bits*, because they snag unwary travelers making them stop for a moment to get unstuck. These bushes are cut and used to encircle villages to keep the cattle in and dangerous animals out.

kwa heri (S) - an expression of farewell meaning *good-bye.*

kwetu Kenya (S) - an expression meaning *in our home in Kenya*.

Maa (M) - the language of the Maasai tribe.

Maasai (M) - the nomadic tribes of the great valleys of central East Africa.

mabati (S) - corrugated sheet metal used for construction, especially for roofing.

maize (S) - a variety of corn, whose kernels are larger and far more chewy than U. S. corn, a staple in Kenya.

malaika (S) - an angel.

mama (S) - mother, often used in conjunction with the name of a woman's eldest daughter, e. g. Mama Stella.

matatu (S) - a small bus. Tatu means *three*, matatu means *three things*. Some say this expression originated because the fare for riding in a small bus is three coins (currently three Kenya shillings in Nairobi). Others say it is so named because *there is always room for three more people* in a matatu.

moran (M) - the young warrior class of the Maasai tribe (equivalent to *il-moran*). These are young men between the ages of fourteen and twenty-five who have satisfactorily completed a formal rite of passage.

mwakari bishwa (S) - an expression meaning *welcome to our country*.

ndio (S) - yes, that is correct.

nimeshiba sana (S) - an expression to communicate that, "I am satisfied."

ni saa nbili ya asubuhi (S) - an expression indicating that the time is 8:00 A.M.. Literal meaning: *there are two hours this morning* [since sunrise].

ni saa ngapi (S) - an expression asking, "What time is it?" Literally: *how many hours are there* [since sunrise]?

nzuri (S) - good, a common reply to the greeting "Habari gani?"

safari (S) - journey. This word has been assimilated into the English language from Kiswahili.

shamba (S) - a small plot of land used for farming, a cultivated field.

Siafu (S) - biting ants, also called Safari Ants.

sopa (M) - a Maasai greeting meaning *hello*.

Swahili (S) - the people from the coast, often having lighter skin than people from the interior.

ugali (S) - corn mush, a common food in Kenya.

uhuru (S) - freedom, as *from the British in 1963*.

undugu (S) - brotherhood.

wageni (S) - strangers.

we mwe ga (K) - a Kikuyu greeting meaning *hello*.

wewe Kikuyu (K) - an expression stating "You are Kikuyu." This is a high complement when extended to someone outside of the tribe.

Photo index

Our group was privileged to receive permission to photograph some of the Kenyan people who we met during our journey. The following index lists the photo subject, the photographer, and the page number of all photos contained in this book.

Chapter 5:

Chapter 6: